THE RISE OF THE

MEANINGFUL
ECONOMY

A MEGATREND WHERE MEANING IS A NEW CURRENCY

MARK DREWELL & BJÖRN LARSSON

ForeSight Press

Finally, a framework for our economic future that we can all embrace. A must read for everyone in business and politics.

Richard Barrett, Chairman & Founder, **The Barrett Values Centre,** Former Values Co-ordinator, World Bank

Already a reality for some, the Meaningful Economy is a compelling prospect for all of us.

Geoff Tudhope, Partner, Fortune 500 CEO Advisors, **Merryck & Co**

The Rise of the Meaningful Economy report is transformational. It showcases what is about to become the new normal. Those who understand that meaning is a new currency, will have first mover advantage and can authentically build deep trust attracting the best customers, employees and investors for the long term.

Misa Lukic, Regional CEO, **Publicis One**

The Rise of the Meaningful Economy is bulls eye in putting words to what I personally experienced working with our global leaders from all continents and sectors (corporate, political, civil society and philanthropists). They came together, year after year, because of shared values in the emerging Meaningful Economy. The Rise of the Meaningful Economy offers powerful insights for corporations to find new ways to create value. It also provides new perspectives for the wealthy and the influential on how to use their resources for the benefit of everyone.

Marilia Bezarra, Former Commitments Director, **Clinton Global Initiative**

The Rise of the Meaningful Economy will wake you up to the new business paradigm that is rapidly emerging. It will make you think in ways you had not thought before about the market and our roles in it as consumers, entrepreneurs and investors. Ways that will be important, not only for the survival of any business, but also for the survival of our society and of our planet.

Tomas Björkman, Founder **Ekskäret Foundation,** Former Chairman EFG Investment Bank & Author; **The Market Myth**

The Rise of the Meaningful Economy is a provocative thought-leadership report that foretells the future that is nearly upon us. In a coherent way, the report ties together what I feel intuitively is happening in the world right now. It offers a sound platform of ideas and analysis about bringing meaning to economic life, followed up with tangible examples of trends, behaviours and organizations we can readily understand. This writing invites us into deeper reflection, further debates, iterative thinking, and experimentation.

Richard Woo, CEO, **The Russel Family Foundation**

The Rise of the Meaningful Economy elegantly articulates what many of us have felt and begun to see - an economy integrating economic and spiritual value and tying together investors, employers, workers and customers in deep and powerful ways. Kudos to The Foresight Group, for identifying meaning as a new currency.

Will Fitzpatrick, Former General Counsel the **Omidyar Network** Advisor to high net worth individuals

The Rise of the Meaningful Economy is your guide to navigating the shift toward relationships over transactions which will dramatically transform our economy. As companies embrace meaning as a core value, engagement will rise, positive impact will grow and customers will amplify your message for you. Meaning is the new money and this book has arrived at the perfect time.

Vicki Saunders, Founder of **SheEO**, the world leading movement for women entrepreneurs and investors

Man's greatest folly is that we ARE our minds and are separate and above the rest; add a healthy dose of money to this delusion and you get a toxic potion. The Rise of the Meaningful Economy brings light and hope to our world by showing us how we can create a new elixir by adding the power of conscious money.

Lawrence Ford, Founder and CEO, **Conscious Capital Wealth Management**

The Rise of the Meaningful Economy identifies with the beginning of the shift we are starting to see in humanity – cutting across generational boundaries and societal beliefs. The value not only comes from the wealth we create, but also from how we invest our time, our resources, our buying power, the people we surround ourselves with and how we plan our futures; all a set of currencies that are based around higher level of consciousness.

Sergio Fernandez de Cordova, Chairman, **PVBLIC Foundation**

The Rise of the Meaningful Economy provides a new lens to look at our emerging future. One which supports the idea that consumers, employees and investors increasingly are putting a premium on companies which are seeking to be relevant to our times.

Tabreez Verjee, Co-founder, **Uprising**

The Rise of the Meaningful Economy timely cuts through swathes of complexity and academic evasions to disclose a concise update on the world economy and important emergent trends. These are pressing times and a necessary revolution is unfolding in business and beyond.

Giles Hutchins, Speaker & Adviser, Author of **Future Fit**

First edition published by ForeSight Press 2017, second edition 2020
ForeSight Group AB, Sveavägen 17, SE 111 57, Stockholm, Sweden

© Copyright Mark Drewell & Björn Larsson

ISBN 978-1-912892-90-7

Also available as an ebook
ISBN 978-1-912892-91-4

Cover: Dejan "Bojke" Bojovic, New Startegy, Belgrade, Serbia
Book design: Klas Kallur, Brinner, Falun, Sweden

Printed and bound by IngramSpark

MEANING IS A NEW CURRENCY

Throughout history and in every culture, people have sought meaning in their lives.

The search for meaning in our existence is therefore nothing new – it is part of the natural condition and perhaps, the ultimate quest for human beings.

The Meaningful Economy on the other hand is something new.

Meaning is increasingly a driver of economic choice – affecting what we buy and from whom, how and where we work, what we do with our capital and how we design and run our organisations.

The rise of the Meaningful Economy is occurring at a tipping point as the number of adults whose circumstances and psychological development orientates them towards living a more meaningful life and expressing that economically.

Consequently meaning is a new lens through which to explore economic value creation.

In short, meaning is a new currency.

MARK DREWELL

mark.drewell@foresight.se

London

BJÖRN LARSSON

bjorn.larsson@foresight.se

Stockholm

ACKNOWLEDGEMENTS

The authors would especially like to thank the following people who contributed to shaping the *The Rise of the Meaningful Economy;*

Alex Novella

Amelie Silfverstolpe

Andrew Dyckhoff

Andy Lam

Ann Dinan

Anne Holm Rannaleet

Professor Ari Kokko

Professor Arnold Smit

Carl-Johan Björklund

Catherine Bachand

Christian Lundberg

Christina Bengtsson

Claire Maxwell

Cleo Sheehan

Dejan Bojovic - Bojke

Dr. Claudius Van Wyk

Dorje Sun

Filip Thorsén

Frank van Beuningen

Geoff Tudhope

Giles Hutchins

Gunnar Michanek

Gustaf Delin

Göran Carstedt

Izeusse Dias Braga Jr

Isak Albihn

Jakob Trollbäck

John North

John Raimondo

John Van Wyk

Klas Kallur

Professor Jonathan Gosling

Lennart Boksjö

Lawrence Ford

Dr. Louis Klein

Louise Hedberg

Louise Yngveson

Marcus Link

Margaret McGovern

Marilia Bezarra

Martin Lindström

Mats Karlsson

Mari Albihn

Marta Sjögren

Misa Lukic

Nick Ellerby

Nicklas Jungegård

Ola Jönsson

Per Molin

Peter Majanen

Peter Willis

Philippe Charas

Richard Barrett

Richard Little

Richard Rudd

Richard Woo

Robert Rubinstein

Sebastian Parsons

Sergio Fernandez de Cordova

Siavash Habibi

Sonja Dragojevic

Sven Atterhed

Tabreez Verjee

Thomas Backteman

Till Gutzen

Tomas Björkman

Tyler Crowley

Ulf Lindberg

Vicki Saunders

Dr. Victoria Hurth

Will Fitzpatrick

Yolanda Drewell

Any errors or omissions remain the sole responsibility of the authors.

INDEX

EXECUTIVE SUMMARY

- the rise of the Meaningful Economy is about meaning driving new economic behaviours offering new opportunities for Value Creation.

Our research has identified that meaning is increasing in importance as a driver of economic choices. This has given rise to a potential megatrend that we have termed The Meaningful Economy.

The principle characteristic of the Meaningful Economy is new behaviours in our four main roles as economic actors:

- » Consumers (what we buy and from who)
- » Employees (how and where we work)
- » Investors (what we do with our capital)
- » Employers (how we design and run our organisations)

These new behaviours, which are integrated and multidimensional, offer new opportunities for value creation.

Here is an excerpt from a composite picture:

I want to work in an organisation where what we do matters, where I can contribute and develop professionally. The world of entrepreneurs and start-ups is more aspirational than that of large organisations. I value time for life beyond work.

When I buy something, I will often consider issues like whether that company does the right thing environmentally, how it shares its profits and whether it pays a fair wage.

I want energy from clean sources. I expect my savings to be invested in things that do well and will create a better future for the world. I am interested in organic food and local craft producers. I upcycle.

Our insight has arisen from a combination of qualitative research and big data analysis.

The rise of the Meaningful Economy is occurring at the tipping point in the number of economically active adults whose circumstances and psychological development orientates them towards seeking to live a more meaningful life and expressing that economically.

Historically only a relatively small elite who had satisfied their survival, safety and security needs could express themselves economically around meaning. They typically did so from the age of forty onwards, as illustrated in the diagram on the levels of psychological development on the next page.

Adapted from Richard Barrett.

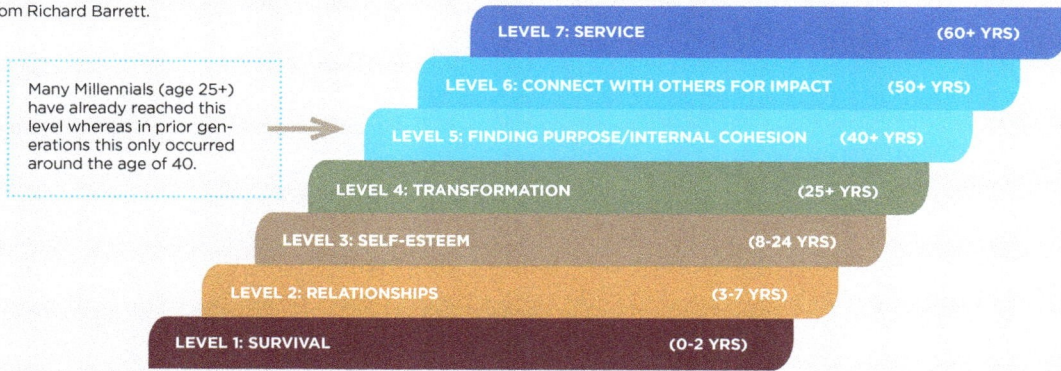

Many Millennials (age 25+) have already reached this level whereas in prior generations this only occurred around the age of 40.

LEVEL 7: SERVICE	(60+ YRS)
LEVEL 6: CONNECT WITH OTHERS FOR IMPACT	(50+ YRS)
LEVEL 5: FINDING PURPOSE/INTERNAL COHESION	(40+ YRS)
LEVEL 4: TRANSFORMATION	(25+ YRS)
LEVEL 3: SELF-ESTEEM	(8-24 YRS)
LEVEL 2: RELATIONSHIPS	(3-7 YRS)
LEVEL 1: SURVIVAL	(0-2 YRS)

THE SEVEN LEVELS OF PSYCHOLOGICAL DEVELOPMENT

- We have reached a tipping point where more people than ever are reaching level 5 and accordingly seeking to live more meaningful lives.

The numbers on each bar represent the typical age at which historically people reach the respective levels of psychological development.

However, in the second half of the twentieth century, an unprecedented and growing number of people have their survival, safety and security needs met and have the capacity and desire to focus on their personal growth. In the diagram above this is the blue levels from "Finding Purpose/Internal Cohesion" upwards.

In terms of a normative developmental journey, this is to be expected amongst Baby Boomers and Generation X who are all now aged 40 years and over. However they are increasingly being joined by growing numbers of Millennials (now aged 25–40) where this focus on meaning appears to be developing earlier in life than in prior generations. The economic impact of this emergent dynamic is enhanced by the fact that Millennials are the largest generation in history in the US – larger at 92 million than the 77 million Baby Boomers.

In terms of economic history, the Meaningful Economy is the new top to a pyramid of value creation

Adapted from Gilmore & Pine.
© 2017 The ForeSight Group.

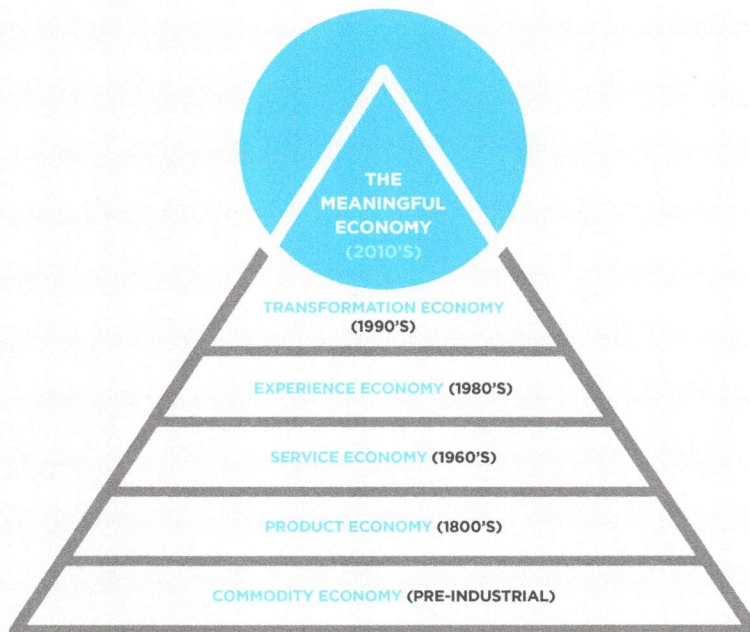

THE
MEANINGFUL
ECONOMY
(2010'S)

TRANSFORMATION ECONOMY
(1990'S)

EXPERIENCE ECONOMY (1980'S)

SERVICE ECONOMY (1960'S)

PRODUCT ECONOMY (1800'S)

COMMODITY ECONOMY (PRE-INDUSTRIAL)

A NEW TOP TO THE PYRAMID OF ECONOMIC VALUE.

Value-added occurs in the transitions from commodities, to products, to services, to experiences, and now to providing meaning.

As always in such a progression, each new level transcends and includes what has gone before. We still have a growing market for commodity-type industrial products while the demand for tailor-made products and services offering us meaning is creating whole new industries in many sectors of the economy.

The Meaningful Economy Lens describes the relationship between new economic behaviours, the driving forces behind them and the consequent opportunities for value creation.

THE MEANINGFUL ECONOMY LENS - NEW OPPORTUNITIES FOR VALUE CREATION.

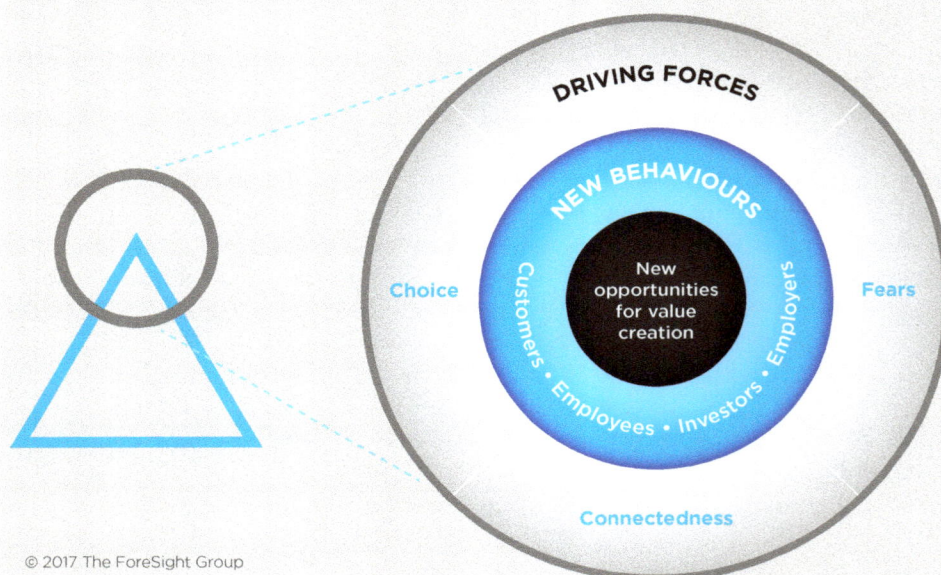

© 2017 The ForeSight Group

Against the background of people seeking to live a more meaning-filled life, we identified **three driving forces that are creating the Meaningful Economy.**

They are **choice, fears and connectedness.**

Individually none are sufficient to create the new behaviours we observe, but **together they have set in motion a flywheel of change.**

1. Choice
The scale and scope of economic choice is unparalleled in human history. Global GDP has tripled in 35 years, the absolute cost of almost everything has fallen and we can access almost anything at any time, anywhere.

2. Fears
We experience our Volatile Uncertain, Complex and Ambiguous (VUCA) world as increasingly unsustainable and in the widest sense, unsustaining.

» **economically,** Jobless Growth is a proxy for the way in which the relationship between our overall economic prosperity and the benefit that it offers, now and in the future, seems to be breaking down.

» **environmentally,** Climate Change embodies our knowledge that the economic system is at best problematic in terms of its environmental impact and at worst, catastrophic.

» **socially,** Mass Migration reinforces our sense that we are not able to address social and societal issues, despite our historically unprecedented high levels of wealth.

3. Connectedness

The internet and digitalisation are powering **new levels of connectedness enabling an unprecedented degree of horizontal (peer-to-peer) communication.** The effect is to inspire, accelerate and scale new ways of thinking and acting. Yet simultaneously it leaves many people feeling more fragmented and consequently seeking more meaningful human relationships.

If choice and fears are the engine, **connectedness is the gearbox transferring power to the wheels of the economy to make it change ever faster.** Five billion mobile subscribers and over eight billion mobile connections give us the ability to connect with everyone, everywhere.

How do we respond to the rise of the Meaningful Economy?

Throughout history and in every culture, people have sought meaning in their lives. The search for meaning in our existence is therefore nothing new – it is part of the natural human condition and perhaps, the ultimate quest for human beings.

The Meaningful Economy on the other hand is something new.

» <u>**For organisations**</u> - the Meaningful Economy offers a new lens through which to create value. It is a new currency.

The lens of Meaning can be used to positively impact every aspect of business - strategy, product and service development, investment choices, approaches to employment and even organisational design.

This development also increases the risk, not only of stranded assets, but even the **risk of stranded business models** that fail to adapt to the rise of meaning as an economic force.

» <u>**For individuals**</u> - the rise of the Meaningful Economy enhances the potential to live a meaning-filled life.

Growing numbers of people can choose more meaningful consumption, more meaningful work and meaningful investment. As business owners and managers we can also choose to run our businesses to create greater meaning for everyone involved.

The leadership challenge in the Meaningful Economy demands a mind-set outside business-as-usual

The rise of the Meaningful Economy is something to which leaders in all organisations will need to pay attention.

A leadership response will be ineffective if framed in the mind-set of business-as-usual. Business-as-usual is characterised by an institutional approach that ensures the incremental success of any established organisation in a (relatively) steady-state system.

To thrive in the Meaningful Economy, organisations need to enhance their ability to create the new, in addition to optimising what already exists.

To create meaning-filled value, organisations and their leaders will increasingly need to focus on being the best <u>for</u> the world rather than the best <u>in</u> the world – to choose relevance over dominance.

It requires the development of creativity and emergence as the core properties to be nurtured and developed. This will not be easy, but the rewards will be great.

The Meaningful Economy can contribute to human progress

Across the world we see traditional leadership being challenged, despised and rejected. Reactionary populism - the world of Trump and Brexit - looks for someone or something to blame for the state of the world. Largely, they blame the Establishment.

The silence of a vibrant positive alternative to reactionary populism is deafening.

Perhaps the Meaningful Economy can help fill that silence as it provides a new narrative around which to build an economic system that serves the common good. It is part of the story of an economic future that moves beyond a focus on GDP growth towards a more holistic view.

The Meaningful Economy supports the achievement of the United Nations Sustainable Development Goals as it puts the whole and individual human being, set in the context of all life and the greater questions of existence, at the centre of the economy rather than the systems and institutions we create.

In 1977, holocaust survivor, neurologist and psychologist **Viktor Frankl** wrote[i]:

> *For too long we have been dreaming a dream from which we are now waking up: the dream that if we just improve the socioeconomic situation of people, everything will be okay, people will become happy.*
>
> *The truth is that as the struggle for survival has subsided, the question has emerged: survival for what?*
>
> *Ever more people today have the means to live, but no meaning to live for.*

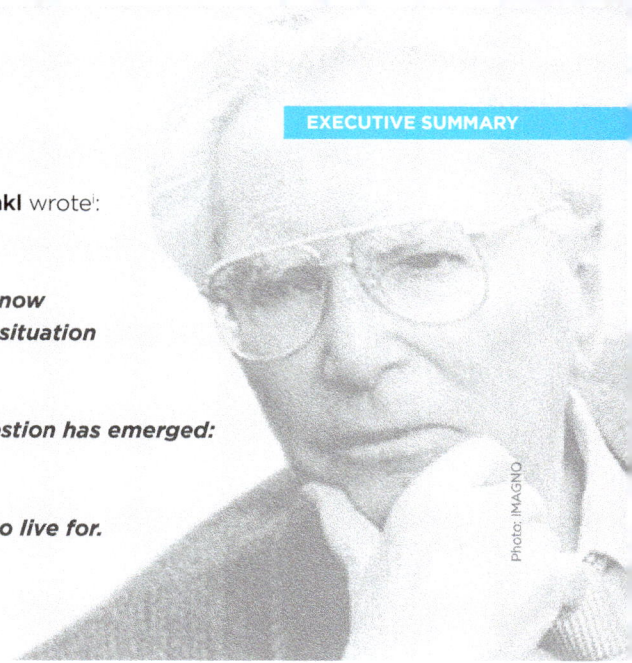

Photo: IMAGNO

The rise of the Meaningful Economy presents the possibility that, through our economic choices, we may be starting to address the issue Frankl so eloquently expressed.

1. OUR RESEARCH JOURNEY

- thirty years of making sense of the future from an economic and business perspective

In the early 1980's the ForeSight Group's founders[i] **Sven Atterhed, Lennart Boksjö** and **Gustaf Delin** collaborated with **John Naisbitt** as he developed his seminal study Megatrends. Naisbitt's book sold 15 million copies worldwide and predicted the information-, knowledge- and network-society of the globaliszed world in which we now live.

The legacy of the ForeSight founders continues today. It inspired ForeSight, senior partner, **Mark Drewell** (formerly Chief Executive of a global coalition of companies and business schools, the Globally Responsible leadership Initiative and prior to that a group executive with South African multinational Barloworld) and CEO, **Björn Larsson** (formerly a Swedish diplomat) to develop their insights on the *Rise of the Meaningful Economy* from their extensive work and involvement in change networks around the world.

These networks **included, the Aspen Institute, the Cambridge Program for Sustainability Leadership, the Clinton Global Initiative (CGI), the Forward Institute, the Global Impact Investing Network (GIIN), the Globally Responsible Leadership Initiative (GRLI), Merryck & Co, NEXUS, PYMWYMIC, the PVBLIC Foundation, the Skoll World Forum and the United Nations Global Compact.**

Initial research which involved interviews with business and thought leaders, revealed a widely-held view that we are moving into a new era.

That sense was deeply felt and shared, even pre-Trump and pre-Brexit. It was described in a myriad of ways and was mirrored not only by those in senior leadership positions, but by people at all levels. Equally striking was that there was no shared clarity on the solutions to the challenges we face, nor a joined-up picture of the future towards which we are moving.

The writer **Yuval Harari** sums up the feeling we found in our conversations across the world:

"

We have lost our story. Humans think in stories. We make sense of the world by telling stories. In the last few decades we had a very simple and attractive story about what is happening in the world.

The story is that the economy is being globalised and the politics are being liberalised. The combination of the two will create prosperity on earth. And we just need to keep on globalising the economy and liberalising the political system and everything will be wonderful.

2016 was the moment when large segments of the population even in the Western world stopped believing in this story. For good or bad reasons, it does not matter, but we as humans do no longer have a story and therefore we do not understand what is happening in the world.

Yuval Harari, Author of *Sapiens*

Big data identified a common trajectory.

Shifting from a qualitative approach to a quantitative analysis, we partnered with **Peter Majanen**, co-founder and Managing Director of the Swedish firm **Quattroporte**[iii]. He brought to the table a fine creative-analytical mind and his expertise in big data[iv]. Quattroporte's proprietary model and database analyses 100 million pages of information and 1 billion tweets.

From a big-data perspective, we explored some 30 emergent trends and movements. We investigated areas as diverse as circular business, the sharing economy, social media, impact investing, organic food, crowd funding and mindfulness. They showed a similar trajectory.[v]

The data analysis confirmed they are statistically correlated. **Figure 1** combines the data from the trends into a single graph.

Visibility Index

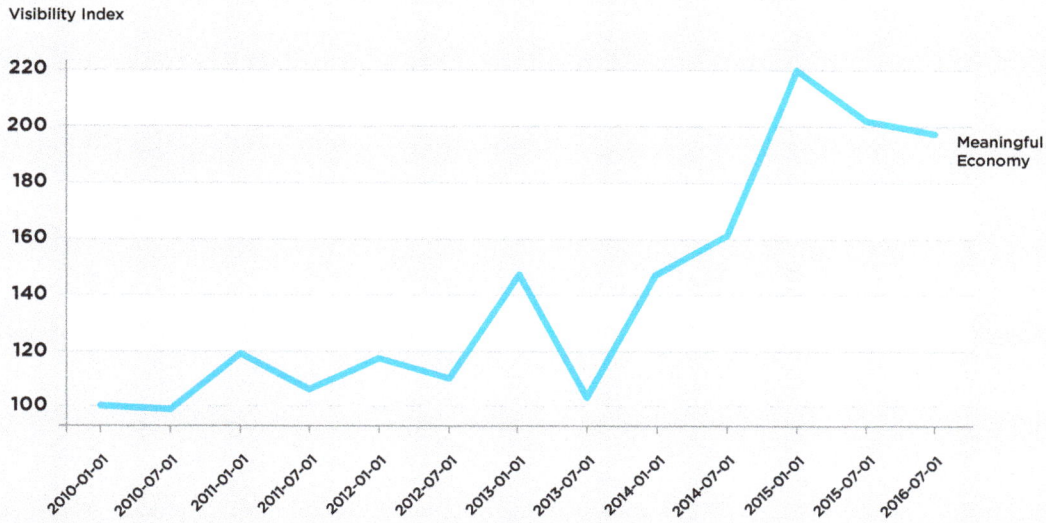

Meaningful
Economy

The graph shows that the phenomenon, which existed in the year 2000, began to emerge around 2010, and then accelerated in 2014.

A micro-trend that only concerned a select few at the Millennium is now developing into something of significance.

We have named this potential new megatrend, the Meaningful Economy.

2. THE MEANINGFUL ECONOMY IS ENABLED BY A TIPPING POINT IN HUMAN DEVELOPMENT

The rise of the Meaningful Economy is occurring at the tipping point in the number of economically active adults whose circumstances and psychological development orientates them towards seeking to live a more meaningful life and expressing that economically.

Historically only a relatively small elite who had satisfied their survival, safety and security needs could express themselves economically around meaning.

However, **in the second half of the twentieth century an unprecedented number of people grew up** with their survival, safety and security needs met and emerged into adulthood **with the capacity and desire to focus on their personal growth.**

This group define our understanding of the so-called Millennial Generation.

This is explained in more detail by **Richard Barrett**[vi], the leading expert on Human Values:

In recent years, I have noticed the early onset of the individuation stage of psychological development among a group of people known as the Millennials. These are children who were born after 1982, live in liberal democracies, and have been raised by well-educated, wealthy parents where they did not encounter any difficulties in learning how to satisfy their deficiency needs.

Research on Millennials in the US suggests they are unlike any other generation in living memory. They are more numerous, more affluent, better educated and more ethnically diverse. They are beginning to manifest a wide array of positive social habits that older Americans no longer associate with youth, including a new focus on teamwork, achievement, modesty and good conduct.

They are optimists: they are happy, content and positive. They are cooperative team players. They accept authority. They trust and feel close to their parents. >>

Photo: www.richardbarrettblog.net

>> *They are smarter than most people think. They believe in the future and see themselves living at the cutting-edge of society.*

In my mind, the Millennials display all the characteristics that I would associate with being brought up by individuated and self-actualized parents; parents who have mastered most of their fears and have found occupations that align with their gifts and talents.

The young people we call Millennials have been loved and cherished, treated fairly and generously, and have been encouraged from an early age to express themselves. In other words, they feel secure in themselves; they have relatively few fears about satisfying their survival, safety and security needs, and many of them are ready and willing to explore their growth needs.

Despite the early onset of the individuation stage of development among Millennials, we cannot yet draw the conclusion that they are on an accelerated path of development. I would rather say they are on an easier or more fluid path of development.

I make this remark for two reasons: first, this group have not struggled to get their needs met and therefore, have fewer fear-based beliefs to overcome; second, they are growing up with a peer group that has a more expansive world view.

Let us not forget, in speaking of Millennials that they are mostly found in affluent democratic nations that have been politically stable for several decades. These are nations that support their populations in meeting their deficiency needs and encourage freedom of thought and freedom of speech. People in these countries are free to explore who they are and satisfy their growth needs.

In understanding the Meaningful Economy it is also useful to consider the typical stages of human development in more detail.

Figure 2 is an adaptation of Richard Barrett's overview of stages of human development.

FIGURE 2:
THE STAGES OF PERSONAL DEVELOPMENT

Adapted from Richard Barrett.

Many Millennials (age 25+) have already reached this level whereas in prior generations this only occurred around the age of 40.

LEVEL 7: SERVICE (60+ YRS)
LEVEL 6: CONNECT WITH OTHERS FOR IMPACT (50+ YRS)
LEVEL 5: FINDING PURPOSE/INTERNAL COHESION (40+ YRS)
LEVEL 4: TRANSFORMATION (25+ YRS)
LEVEL 3: SELF-ESTEEM (8-24 YRS)
LEVEL 2: RELATIONSHIPS (3-7 YRS)
LEVEL 1: SURVIVAL (0-2 YRS)

The numbers on each bar represent the typical age at which historically people reach the respective levels of psychological development.

From birth development into early adulthood we move from survival, through developing the capacity to be in relationships with others, to a teenage focus on self-esteem and then into a journey of transformation from the mid-twenties into our thirties.

For the Meaningful Economy, the relevant part of the life journey from survival to service is the last three stages shaded blue.

Historically these stages have emerged as people enter mid-life (their 40's) and start to feel more deeply that their existence is not infinite. With that, they orientate themselves towards a more meaning-filled life where they seek to live with more internal cohesion, expressed around finding a purpose. Then around that purpose and cohesion they will connect with others and ultimately move to a state of service (typically in their 60's).

This "traditional" view is contained in the age numbers above each of the last four steps of the ladder in **Figure 2.**

What Barrett has observed is that a growing numbers of Millennials are reaching the three blue levels earlier in life. We also found anecdotal evidence that this is the case, both in our study and as we have begun to share its findings. Millennials recognise this pattern amongst their peers and older generations identify it in their children and in younger members of society around them.

According to a recent Goldman Sachs study[vii], Millennials are the largest generation in history in America (figure 3).

Comprising 92 million people, they are more numerous even than the 77 million baby boomers.

Today, Millennials range in age between approximately twenty-five and forty. This makes them increasingly important in shaping the economic agenda.

US POPULATION (MILLIONS)

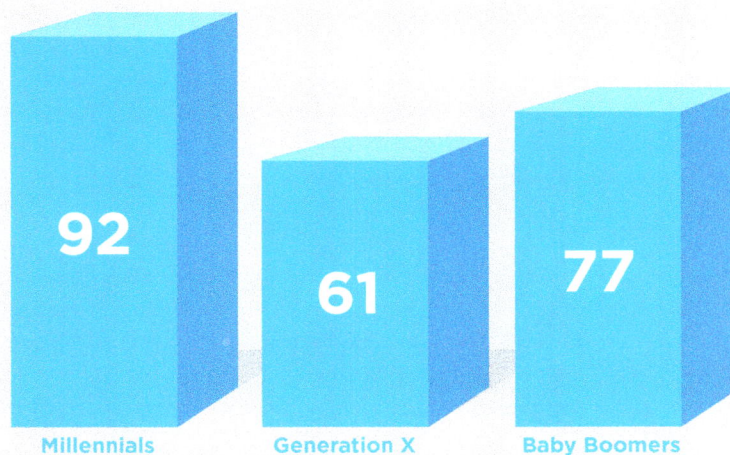

FIGURE 3:
MILLENIALLS ARE THE LARGEST GENERATION IN US HISTORY.

92 — Millennials
61 — Generation X
77 — Baby Boomers

Source:
Goldman Sachs

These "Millennials" combine with those in older generations whose personal development has already reached a stage of orientating their life choices around more meaningful activity.

Whilst we have been unable to find hard data on the absolute numbers of people involved, our conclusion is nonetheless that the scale of this development is sufficient to create a tipping point[viii] which is giving rise to the Meaningful Economy.

From a Meaningful Economy perspective, Millennials are a generation who have moved into a phase of life where they are becoming economically powerful at precisely the time that three driving forces have come together to set in motion a flywheel of change.

These driving forces are Choice, Fears and Connectedness. They will be described fully in chapter four of this report.

However it is important to highlight how the Millennial relationship to these driving forces differs from the average across all adults:

» **Millennials experience choice as Normal**
   Millennials have experienced the power of ever-growing choice as being "normal" in that it has been around since their childhood, either as a reality amongst those in a comfortable economic situation, or as aspirations amongst those less well-off.

» **Millennials experience our fears as based on fact, not opinion**
   Millennials are most likely to experience the effect of our fears that create the desire for new behaviours because they are the first generation to grow up confronting growing evidence that the economic system built in the 20th century was not going to inevitably produce wellbeing for all.

   At school, Millennials were taught the basics of how we are affecting the ecosystems in which we live, creating climate change, making species extinct on an unprecedented scale, destroying rainforests etc. Having learnt about these subjects, they become deeply ingrained facts rather than just interesting new ideas.

   By contrast their parents experienced the defining issue of their formative years as being the conflict between capitalism and communism. Millennials' parents also grew up in a world where the damaging relationship between the economic system and nature was at the cutting edge of our understanding.

   It was only in 1970 that the first serious quantitative analysis, **Limits to Growth,** modelled the consequences of the trajectory we were on as being the destruction of the natural systems on which we depend for our survival. This "knowing" is having a similar affect as the consequences of the prior generation (Gen X born 1965–1980) growing up and learning about the dangers of smoking, which founded the understanding for sweeping changes to smoking regulations across the world as they grew into adulthood.

» **Millennials are connected as Digital Natives**
   The term digital native was coined and popularized by education consultant **Marc Prensky** in his 2001 article **Digital Natives, Digital Immigrants**. Prensky did not strictly define the digital native, but in common use it has come to mean those born after 1980 who have grown up in a world of digital technology. This has created a different relation-

ship amongst Millennials to technology than that of prior generations. In every conceivable aspect of life, Millennials see the Internet and Digitalisation as normal, natural and an extension of who they are, and how they function.

The preferences of Millennials are beginning to set the terms for the attractive life style of the future.

In so doing, they are also creating conditions under which similar outlooks held by people in other (older) generations can become more visible. This widens the concept of Millennials as a generation only, to **Millennialism** as a mind-set. **Millennialism incorporates people from older generations who share a Millennial outlook.**

Our analysis characterises Millennialism as being exemplified by the following composite profile:

❝

I want to work for an organisation where what we do matters. Where we have a real and articulated sense of purpose and where I can contribute and develop professionally. I like to work collaboratively rather than being told what to do by the boss.

The world of entrepreneurs and start-ups is more aspirational than that of big corporations. None of my most talented friends really want to work in large firms – and especially those seen as socially extractive such as professional services companies or banks.

I value time for life outside work and I like to participate in reflective practices such as mindfulness. I'm comfortable in a gig economy where I go from project-to-project rather than having a full time job with one company.

When I buy something, I will often consider issues like whether that company pays its fair share of taxes, does the right thing environmentally, how it shares its profits and whether it pays a fair wage and its fair share of taxes where it makes its money.

I prefer to get my energy from clean sources. I don't want my pension invested in fossil fuel companies and I increasingly expect it to be invested in things that do well and will create a better future for the world.

I am interested in organic food and local craft producers. I upcycle.

In the next section we set out a working definition of the Meaningful Economy.

3. A DEFINITION OF THE MEANINGFUL ECONOMY

We have created, with the input of **Richard Barrett**, a working definition of the Meaningful Economy by adapting the work on meaning of the eminent psychologist **Roy Baumeister**[ix].

In the Meaningful Economy, economic choices are made based on a preference for actions which have the following properties:
- » They **are informed by sense of higher purpose** that orientates towards the common good rather than self(ish) interest
- » They are **underpinned by the most positive values** we share as human beings
- » They **make a positive contribution** towards building a global caring society
- » They **provide a basis for creating a sense of well-being** and fulfilment in our lives.

This working definition is directional and not definitive. The authors welcome efforts by others on its improvement.

The Meaningful Economy points towards a new kind of development where economic activity is restored to its role as an enabler of progress, not the outcome.

Given that it is a bottom-up movement, it will take policy-makers time to understand it and then create a context in which its development is supported and accelerated. The benefits of doing so are, we believe, significant. They may provide the seeds of a new narrative beyond the discourse which creates the impression that the only choices we have are those of regulation versus more free market capitalism.

Understanding the Meaningful Economy requires a wider perspective than a discussion focused primarily on the arena of what an organisation delivers – its products and services.

It is natural for the business reader, informed by the language of neo-liberal economics and the world's +20 000 business schools, to assume that business-related matters will be couched in a particular way.

The Meaningful Economy, to be of any use, has to step outside this norm, because it seeks to address the realities beyond an economics based in theories of utilitarian rational choice. It recognises that people locate value in what they perceive as meaningful in their different roles as customers or consumers, employees, investors or owners of companies.

Meaning extends the concept of value beyond a utilitarian value-for-money approach and allows for the incorporation of cultural, environmental, physical, mental and spiritual wellbeing as important aspects of what constitutes value. It is about people's lives becoming more "whole".

4. A NEW LEVEL WITHIN WHICH TO SEEK ECONOMIC VALUE

Meaning adds a new perspective to the historical developmental framework of economic value created by **Gilmore and Pine**[x].

This framework, set out as a pyramid in **Figure 4**, identified a hierarchy of economic evolution.

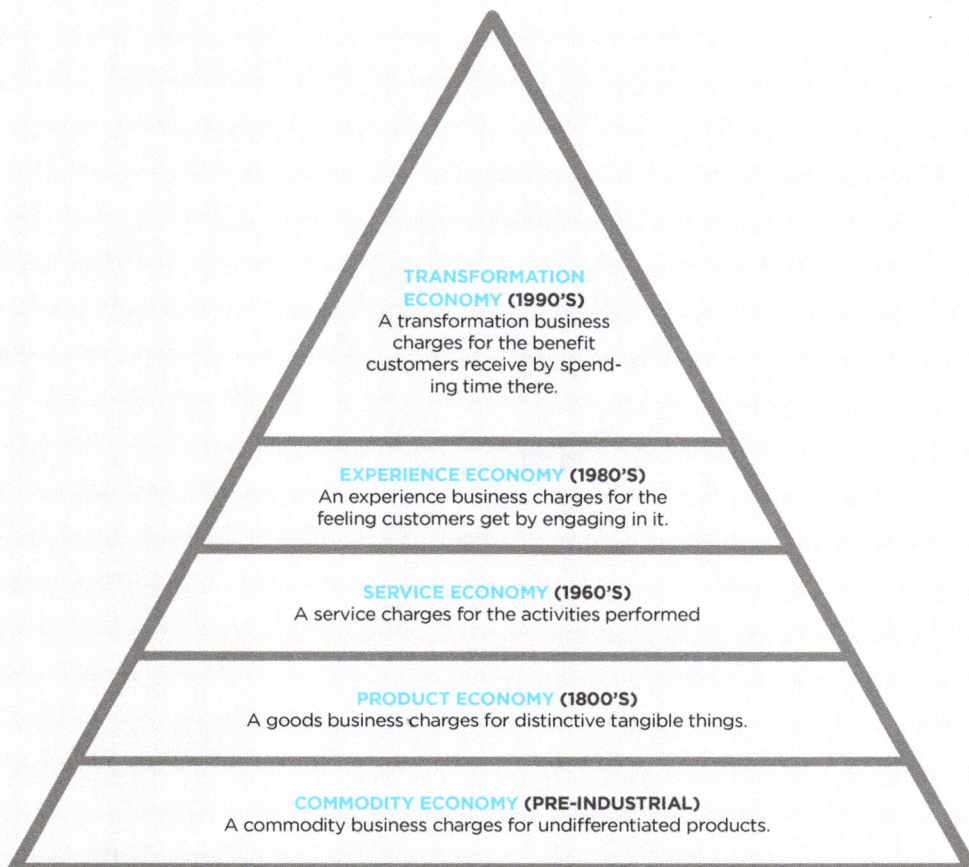

FIGURE 4:
JAMES GILMORE AND JOE PINE'S HIERARCHY OF ECONOMIES.

TRANSFORMATION ECONOMY (1990'S)
A transformation business charges for the benefit customers receive by spending time there.

EXPERIENCE ECONOMY (1980'S)
An experience business charges for the feeling customers get by engaging in it.

SERVICE ECONOMY (1960'S)
A service charges for the activities performed

PRODUCT ECONOMY (1800'S)
A goods business charges for distinctive tangible things.

COMMODITY ECONOMY (PRE-INDUSTRIAL)
A commodity business charges for undifferentiated products.

Each level, developing over time, transcends and includes the prior levels while shifting the arena in which maximum value is created. Economies within this framework interact in a complex eco-system. New developments occur toward the top of the pyramid while the more basic, yet still important, parts (for instance raw materials production in the commodity economy) are found further down.

In their famous case study of Starbucks, Gilmore and Pine showed how the company, by creating a genuine experience in their coffee shops could charge significantly more for their cup of coffee than an ordinary café or a store selling coffee in the grocery aisles. At Starbucks, customers were willing to pay a premium price for a well-designed experience. The lowest value-add in the chain is sacks of coffee beans sold in the market wholesale. The higher up in the hierarchy, the more value can be generated.

Since the original study, an additional layer was added to the pyramid of value. This is the **Transformation Economy** in which value is found in products and services that develop individuals and societies. A strong experience is no longer enough; the experience also has to contribute to positive development.

Two examples of the Transformation Economy are the expansion of the exercise industry and organic food; both make you feel better at the time of consumption and help develop better health in the long run.

It has been almost 20 years since the Transformation Economy was presented as the pinnacle of progression in the relationship between companies and their customers. We are ready to move on.

The rise of the Meaningful Economy not only adds a new layer to the top of this pyramid (Figure 5), but also adds a different quality to value creation.

FIGURE 5:
THE MEANINGFUL ECONOMY ADDS A NEW PEAK TO THE PYRAMID, CREATING NEW OPPORTUNITIES FOR VALUE CREATION.

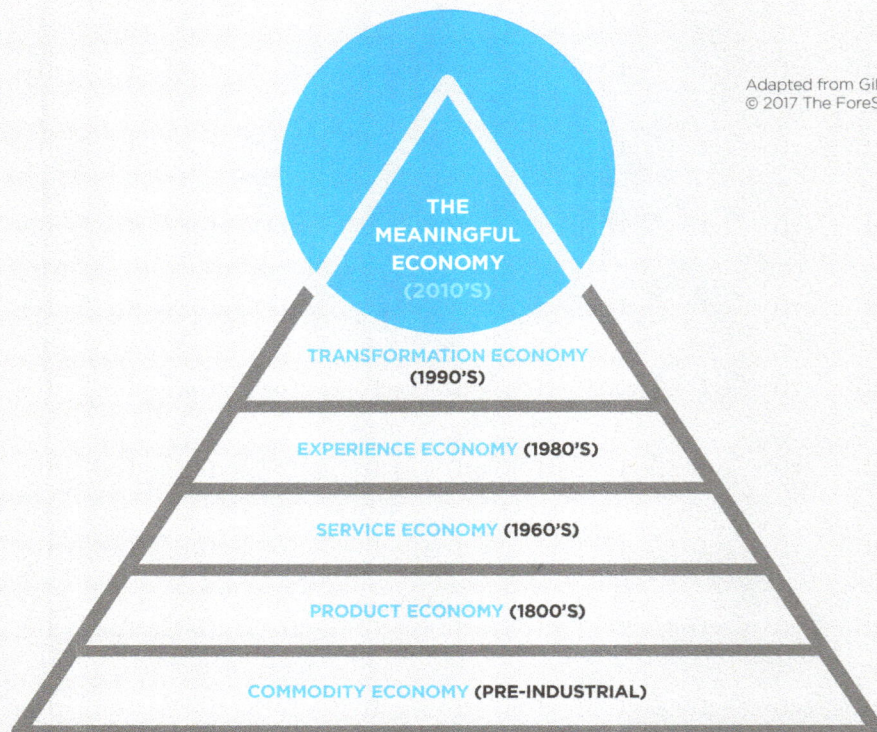

Adapted from Gilmore & Pine
© 2017 The ForeSight Group

THE MEANINGFUL ECONOMY (2010'S)

TRANSFORMATION ECONOMY (1990'S)

EXPERIENCE ECONOMY (1980'S)

SERVICE ECONOMY (1960'S)

PRODUCT ECONOMY (1800'S)

COMMODITY ECONOMY (PRE-INDUSTRIAL)

How that happens is a sea-change in the perspective of what matters in economic decision-making.

Value creation is now powered not only by what an organisation provides to its customers, but also by a much wider dynamic located amongst other stakeholders and in areas outside the realm of products and services. It is a felt experience and worldview that looks for something different.

In the Meaningful Economy higher value is created where people feel more complete as a result of their economic actions. In the broadest sense, organisations charge for --- creating meaning.

In the Meaningful Economy conventional ideas of brand management and reputation building are not sufficient.

Value is derived from every aspect of what a company does and from being attuned to the world in which people would like to live.

This cannot be addressed within a communication framework alone. It is about the underlying behaviours of an organisation and the system within which it operates and thrives.

5. UNDERSTANDING THE MEANINGFUL ECONOMY LENS

The Meaningful Economy offers a lens for value creation. It comprises three sets of building blocks:

» the driving forces that bring it into being against the background of a tipping point in personal development discussed in chapter 2

» new behaviours that these driving forces create

» new opportunities for value creation now and in the future

Figure 6 summarizes the dynamic within the Meaningful Economy from a systems perspective.

The Meaningful Economy is emerging through the interaction between three driving forces:

» unprecedented levels of Choice

» our response to the Fears that have developed as a result of the failures

» of the economic system to deliver the results which we would like

» the degree of our Connectedness creating unfiltered horizontal communication through the enabling power of the internet and digitalisation.

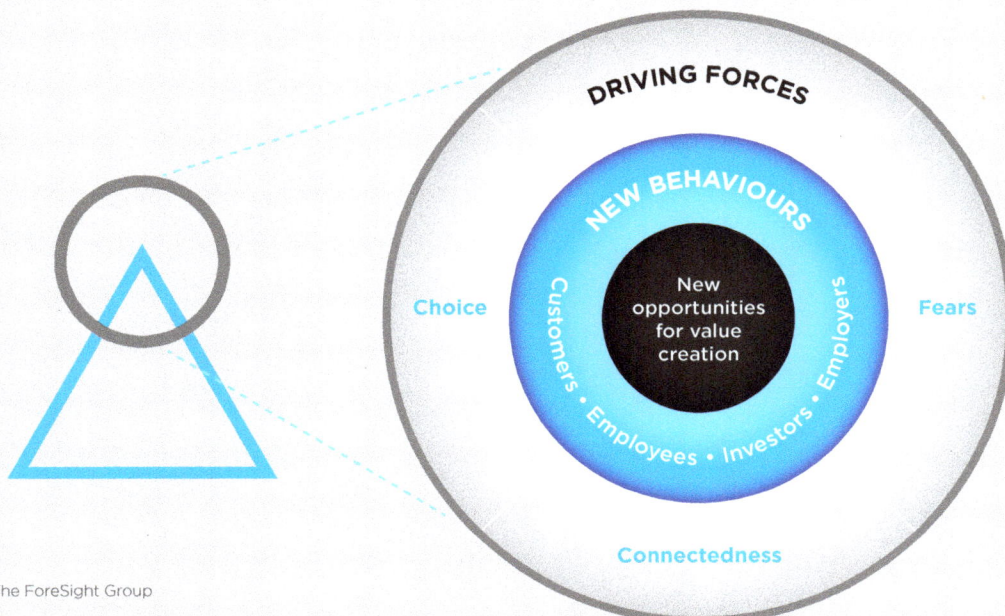

FIGURE 6:
THE MEANINGFUL ECONOMY LENS: THREE DRIVING FORCES, STIMULATE NEW ECONOMIC BEHAVIOURS, WHICH IN TURN OFFER NEW OPPORTUNITIES FOR VALUE CREATION.

Each of the three driving forces individually would not be a sufficient condition for the rise of the Meaningful Economy, but by existing at the same time, they interact and work together to create the conditions under which it can emerge.

The interaction between the three driving forces creates New Behaviours.

These new behaviours are exhibited in the various direct economic roles that individuals perform – being a customer, an employee, an employer or an investor. There is a fifth economic role which we play as enablers of economic activity through the societal process of economic policies, regulations and laws. This is our economic role as citizens. While we recognise its importance, we have chosen not to assess it in any detail in this analysis.

The consequences of these new behaviours are that they create New Opportunities for value creation.

In the following sections we explore each of these elements in more detail.

NÄRINGSLIV

the Swedish word
for enterprise,
literally means

NURTURING LIFE

6. DRIVING FORCES OF THE MEANINGFUL ECONOMY

Three driving forces of Choice, Fears and Connectedness operate together to create the Meaningful Economy and are the first building block of the Lens.

In this section we explore each of them in turn in order to understand their nature and power.

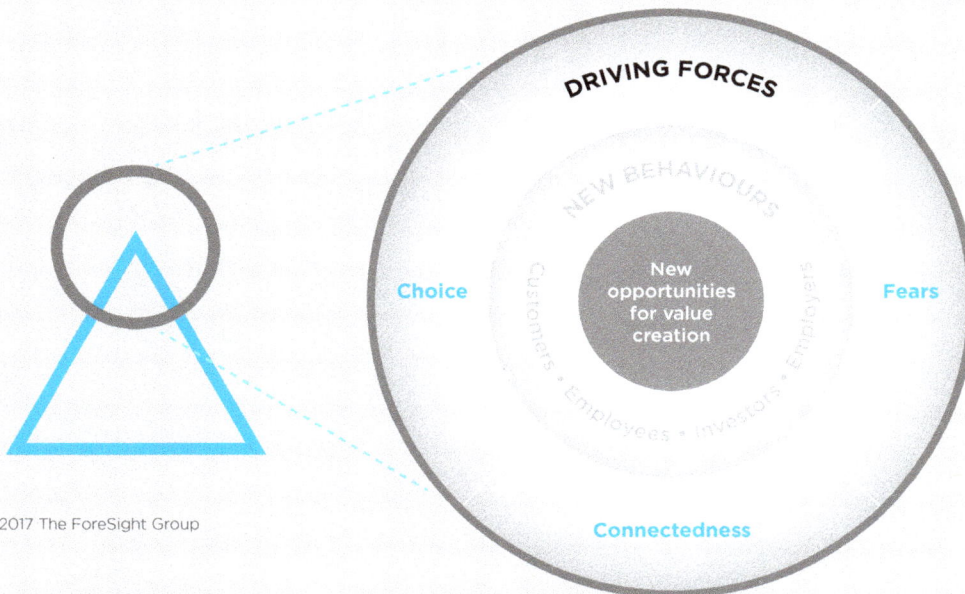

DRIVING FORCES

NEW BEHAVIOURS

Choice

Fears

New opportunities for value creation

Customers • Employees • Investors • Employers

Connectedness

© 2017 The ForeSight Group

6.1 Choice unlocks the possibility of new behaviours

More people have a greater ability to choose how they live their economic lives than at any time in history.

Choice is at the heart of a market economy. The ability to choose between different products and services defines our consumer society.

The unprecedented degree of choice available today compared with the past has four aspects:

a) Choice through scale

....

The unprecedented scale of economic activity in the world gives an ever-growing portion of the global population the ability to choose how they live their economic lives. This remains true, notwithstanding an equally unprecedented inequality of income and wealth distribution.

In the last 35 years alone, global GDP has almost tripled in real terms[xi]:

1980:	2015:
27.8	**74.5**
TRILLION	TRILLION
US$	**US$**

Even at the bottom end of the economic spectrum the number of people having some degree of economic choice has grown dramatically - in the decade beginning in 2002, the proportion of the world's population living below the poverty line dropped by half from 26% to 13%.

b) Choice through accessibility

....

In 1980 a European family who wished to prepare Sushi could only have done so if they lived in one of the major cities where it may have been possible to buy wasabi, nori (dried sea-weed), rice wine vinegar and other required ingredients in a speciality store. Today such items are usually available in most major supermarket chains and even in small towns.

This pattern is repeated in most categories of food and across many other sectors.

It is also as true for business-to-business supply chain purchases as for the retail sector. And if an item is not available physically locally, it is usually available the next day from an online store.

Practically, anyone can increasingly buy anything, anywhere and at any time.

The story in services is similar, and best exemplified by the airline industry. Discount airlines allow the opportunity for the traveller to travel internationally and between regional airports across continents. More routes are added every year. This is not only a developed world phenomenon as nowhere has the growth of choice in affordable airline travel been more rapid than in India and China.

c) Choice through lower cost

In absolute and in real terms the cost of most goods and services has fallen and continues to fall. Nowhere is this more visible than in technology. In 1980, a portable colour TV cost just under US$ 600. Adjusting for inflation that is the equivalent of US$1,715 today. By comparison a 42 inch smart LED TV currently costs less than US$300.

Simply put, a modestly affluent consumer with two children who could have afforded one portable colour TV in 1980, can now put a large flat-screen TV in every bedroom in the house as well as one in the kitchen and one in the lounge.

That same family can also contemplate choices that were unimaginable a generation ago in terms of, for example, vacations.

Not only has the development of the airline industry allowed for greater choice of destinations, but the cost of travel has fallen sharply. In the US, the average round-trip domestic journey price fell from $443 in 1979 to $281in 2015. This figure includes all classes of travel. When considering the impact of discount airlines, the effect is even more remarkable.

In 1986 the first **RyanAir** return flights from London to Dublin were priced at £99. This was less than half the then **British Airways** price of £208.

Today that same flight is available for £40.

Taking into account inflation, the 1986 BA flight cost more than 12 times the equivalent trip today.

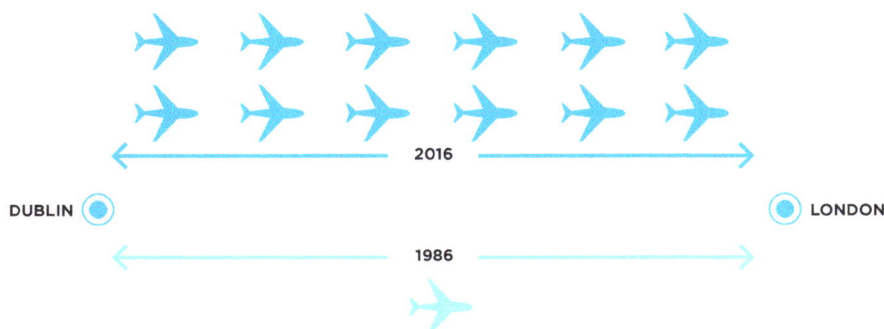

d) Choice through basic infrastructure and medical advances

Choice is enabled not only by the relationship between the ability to purchase a given level of products and services, but also the extent to which the society has the infrastructure and systems to meet more fundamental needs.

Johan Norberg[xii] notes that even relatively poor people today have better health than even the richest in the past.

The 2009 swine flu pandemic threatened to become catastrophic, but scientists sequenced the genome of the virus within a day and produced a vaccine in less than six months.

Simple technologies such as clean water and indoor plumbing are now available to 68% of the world's population (up from 24% in 1980).

By contrast, in the 17th century, one of the wealthiest men of his day, the Sun King Louis XIV had to rely on chamber pots for the needs of his Royal Court at Versailles (pictured below).

The Palace of Versailles was a marvel of its age, but did not have basic sewerage or plumbing.

First built by Louis XIII in 1623 as a hunting lodge, it was extensively remodelled and expanded by Louis XIV. In 1682, he proclaimed the palace his principal residence and the seat of the government of the Kingdom of France.

The Palace of Versailles

Photo: Ilya Malnikov/Courtesy of Harper

> *We are right now living in the best of times in human history.*
>
> *More people die from eating too much, than from eating too little.*
>
> *More people die of old age, than from infectious diseases.*
>
> *More people commit suicide, than die from crime, terrorism and war taken together.*

Yuval Harari, Author of *Sapiens*

> " We are at the most dangerous moment in the development of humanity. We now have the technology to destroy the planet on which we live, but have not yet developed the ability to escape it.

Professor Stephen Hawking, 2017[xiii]

6.2 Fears provide the reason to change behaviour

Our fears stimulate the search for alternatives to established norms.

They create the potential for new behaviours in the context of one or more of what **Nick Ellerby** of the **Oasis School for Human Relations** describes as the five triggers for change:

1. A change in the life phase you are in
2. An external event which changes your focus
3. A spiritual awakening
4. The experience of pain including through dysfunctional patterns
5. A conscious decision to develop

Gradually and inexorably over the past twenty years, there has been a growing recognition that despite enormous progress in many areas, the world is not on an especially positive trajectory.

In our own work at the **ForeSight Group**, a decade ago we would host workshops to explore the idea that "the system is broken" and expect this to be met with an initially hostile reaction. Today, we find that the conversation frequently assumes that this statement is correct and then moves quickly on to discuss *why the system is broken* and *what should be done.*

Our research has identified three main issues that embody our collective experience of a Volatile, Uncertain, Complex and Ambiguous (VUCA) world:

a. Jobless growth
b. Climate change
c. Mass migration

These three issues provide the context for a driving force of fears about the present and the future, creating the stimulus for the rise of the Meaningful Economy. We will now consider each in turn.

a) Fear of Jobless Growth

In 2013 **Carl Frey and Michael Osborne** published their detailed study of the extent to which different jobs were susceptible to computerization.[xiv]

The two Oxford University academics looked at 702 occupations. They reached the startling conclusion that 47% of US employment was at risk from the effects of computerization.

They are not unique in identifying a looming problem.

Erik Brynjolfsson, co-author the *The Second Machine Age*, sees a parallel between agriculture a century ago and manufacturing today. In 1900 42% of the US workforce was employed in agriculture compared with 2% today.[xv] As the director of **MIT's Initiative on the Digital Economy**, he is amongst a growing number of tech gurus who recognize the problems evolving from the effect of technology on employment.

These insights are the reason why, in Silicon Valley, the heartland of entrepreneurial wealth creation, the call for a **Universal Basic Income** (UBI) is on the rise.[xvi] UBI, also known as a Citizens Income, is being championed by people like **Tesla** inventor **Elon Musk.** UBI envisages every human being receiving an income, irrespective of whether they work. Ethically, this is founded on the view that given that there is enough wealth for every human being to flourish, we should do a better job of ensuring it is shared around and in so doing, we will increase spending power and create more economic activity, not less.

The call for UBI in the tech sector is also a symptom of the way in which those on the edge of techno-economic development are amongst the first to see a fundamental decoupling of economic growth from new work opportunities. Since the industrial revolution, new jobs have historically replaced those destroyed by progress. This appears to be no longer the case. The world of work that can provide progressive opportunities and sustainable, secure incomes for a global population is disappearing under technical innovation. This is occurring notwithstanding the fact that as we live longer (with more needs) and have more money to spend, so new opportunities should be created.

Robotic arms perform spot welds on the chassis of a van under assembly at a Ford assembly plant in Claycomo, Missouri. Photo: Reuters.

From the rise of robot pizza delivery to the automation of accounting functions through online small business Apps, the spectre of a world in which reducing prospects for meaningful paid work as a norm, loom ever larger in the public consciousness.

Jobless growth forms part of a picture that includes an ever-increasing portion of wealth accumulating in the hands of a smaller portion of the population.

The most powerful illustration of this was a report presented at the January 2017 **World Economic Forum** in Davos which concluded that the eight richest men in the world control the same wealth as the poorest half of the entire global population[xvii].

Much of this is seen as a market failure in which the economic system is not delivering the results that were assumed would flow from growing GDP. In the past, to some extent, any market failure was partially obscured by the prospect of upward migration into professional work. However jobless growth threatens many roles which were previously capable of offering skilled and consequently better remunerated employment. Much of the value in the economy increasingly resides in intellectual property and in digital data, which are by nature alienated from employees and customers, subject to value-adding by algorithm and software design, and consequently primarily appropriated by companies (for their shareholders with the effect of further concentrating wealth).

These fears are driven not only by the prospects of work, but what can be bought even if you have a good job.

In the United Kingdom for example, the term **Generation Rent** is used to identify the reality for many Millennials that there is no mechanism, given the price of property, for them ever to own their own homes.

> *The very design of our economies and the principles of our economics have taken us to this extreme, unsustainable and unjust point. Our economy must stop excessively rewarding those at the top and start working for all people.*

Oxfam Report January 2017

Generation Rent is a manifestation of a structural problem in the economy. Most people access the opportunity for economic success through their wages. In the US, productivity increased by 80.4% between 1973 and 2011, but the real hourly compensation of the median worker went up by only 10.7%. The bulk of the benefit flowed somewhere else. Since the trend everywhere has been to reduce taxation, it was not to society at large. The benefit flowed instead primarily to those with control over financial resources - to providers of capital and to wealth holders.

Wealth has gushed up, not trickled down.

At a personal level, people also experience an **increasingly unpredictable work life and with it a falling sense of income security.**

The idea that a career is even possible is no longer the norm amongst the current generation of school leavers notwithstanding that many of their parents still cling on to the idea.

Jobless growth takes to skies: The **Ehang-184** is the world's first passenger aerial drone taxi prototype. Following successful test flights, Guangzhou-based **EHANG** is being trialled in Dubai in 2017.

Photo: www.ehang.com

b) Fear of Climate Change

Fears about the impact of our economic system on the environment have come to focus on the effects of burning fossil fuels on the average temperature of the planet. The evidence is so overwhelming that Pre-traumatic Stress Syndrome is now emerging as a phenomenon amongst climate scientists whose work puts them into contact daily with the reality of melting glaciers, sea level rise, increasing weather volatility and its consequences for humanity.[xviii]

Given that we now have nearly a generation of young adults across the world that have, in their basic education, been exposed to the knowledge of the ways in which our economic system is affecting the natural world, it is perhaps unsurprising that this is a major factor in creating the fears which create the conditions for behavioural change.

In addition to what is already happening, the future prognosis based on our current trajectory is extremely negative.

Our current economic models and development patterns feed a relentless demand to consume more of the natural system on which we depend for our existence.

As a consequence many people feel a deep sense of helplessness.

By 2030, according to **Cambridge University**[xix] the combination of population growth and rising incomes will result in what they have called **"the Perfect Storm"**:
   a. 50% increase in demand for food
   b. 50% increase in demand for energy
   c. 30% increase in demand for water

The Cambridge analysis highlights that we need to produce more food in the next 40 years, than we have produced during the last 8 000 years.

In addition to climate change and carbon emissions, the Millennial Generation's embedded understanding of other environmental issues confronts them with ethical dilemmas that their (relatively ignorant) parents have not had to face.

These are most powerfully presented in the **Stockholm Resilience Centre's Planetary Boundaries Framework (Figure 7).**[xx] The framework identifies 9 Earth systems processes which have boundaries that, to the extent that they are not crossed, mark the safe zone for humanity. This is a precondition for sustainable development.

The Framework was first published in 2009 report and presented to the General Assembly of the **Club of Rome** in Amsterdam. Its findings were subsequently published as the featured article in a special edition of Nature. In 2015, an updated paper was published in Science.

Figure 7 shows that for two of the planetary boundaries we have already gone beyond the threshold of safety. These are Change in Biosphere Integrity (which combines biodiversity loss and species extinction) and Biogeochemical Flows (phosphorus and nitrogen cycles). Other boundaries are in imminent danger of being crossed. We have succeeded in reversing the negative trend for Atmospheric Ozone Depletion through concerted global action showing that the collapse of the safe operating space is not inevitable.

> *Transgressing a boundary increases the risk that human activities could inadvertently drive the Earth System into a much less hospitable state, damaging efforts to reduce poverty and leading to a deterioration of human wellbeing in many parts of the world, including wealthy countries.*

Professor **Will Steffen,** lead author, **2015 Planetary Boundaries Update**

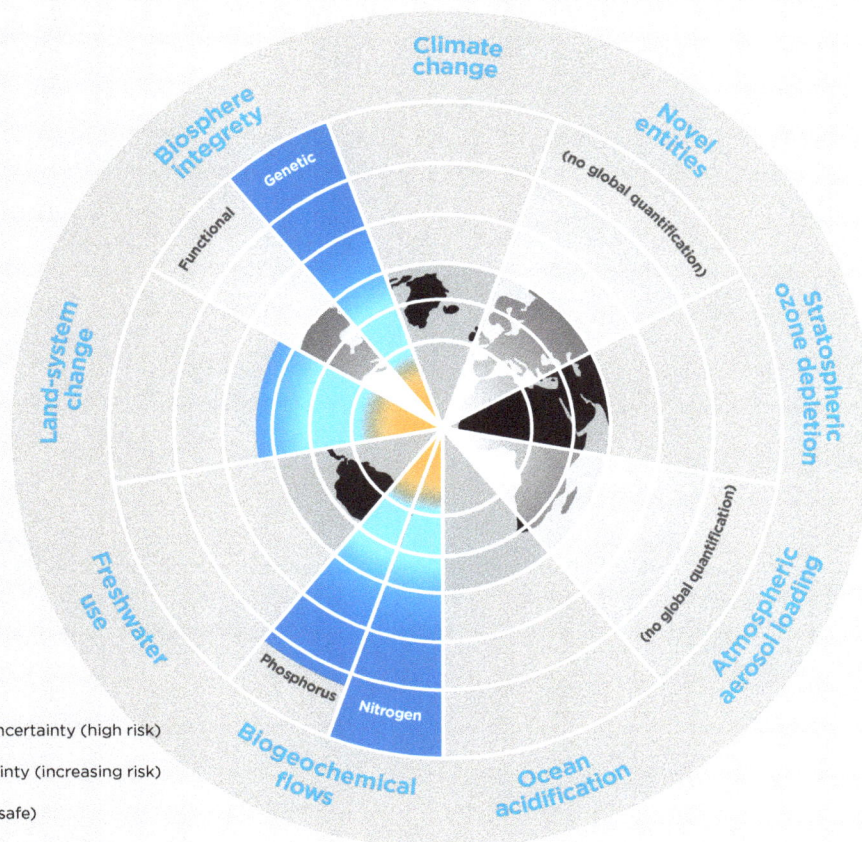

FIGURE 7:
SUMMARY OF THE 2015 PLANETARY BOUNDARIES UPDATE - THE LONG TERM PROGNOSIS FOR NATURE BEING ABLE TO SUSTAIN THE CURRENT GLOBAL POPULATION IS POOR AND GETTING WORSE UNLESS WE ACT.

Source: Steffen et al. Planetary boundaries: Guiding human development on a charging planet. Science. 16 January 2015.

Illustration graphic adapted by ForeSight Group.

Legend:
- Beyond zone of uncertainty (high risk)
- In zone of uncertainty (increasing risk)
- Below boundary (safe)
- Boundary not yet quantified

c) Fear of Mass Migration

In 2015 alone, more than one million migrants and refugees crossed into Europe primarily from the Middle East. It sparked a crisis as countries struggled to cope with the influx, and is creating division in the EU over how best to deal with resettling people.[xxi]

When human beings become stressed, the temptation to find someone to blame can easily become endemic. Migration stimulates such fears.

Migration includes both cross border migration (the kind that comes quickest to mind for many people) and urbanization (the structural shift from rural to urban living).

According to the **United Nations,** 54% of the global population is now urban with that percentage growing every year. Fears around migration are also being fed by continued global population growth.

Factors driving migration include:
- » the general desire to search for a better life beyond poverty
- » escaping the consequences of failed and failing states and zones of conflict
- » the impact of climate change and other environmental degradation

For many, mass migration is also seen as a negative consequence of globalization and the opening up of markets to free trade in labour as well as goods and services.

On top of the insecurity migration creates, there is a sense even in the richest nations of a diminishing lack of political will and/or the ability to provide basic infrastructure, let alone effective support systems for the young, the old and those left behind.

The doughnut of social and ecological interconnection

In 2012, new thinking by **Kate Raworth** combined the planetary boundaries ecological work with twelve dimensions of the social foundation derived from internationally agreed minimum social standards identified in the work done to develop the **United Nations Sustainable Development Goals.**

Between social and planetary boundaries lies an environmentally safe and socially just space in which humanity can thrive **(Figure 8)**. This approach recognises the inter-relationship between social and environmental dynamics.

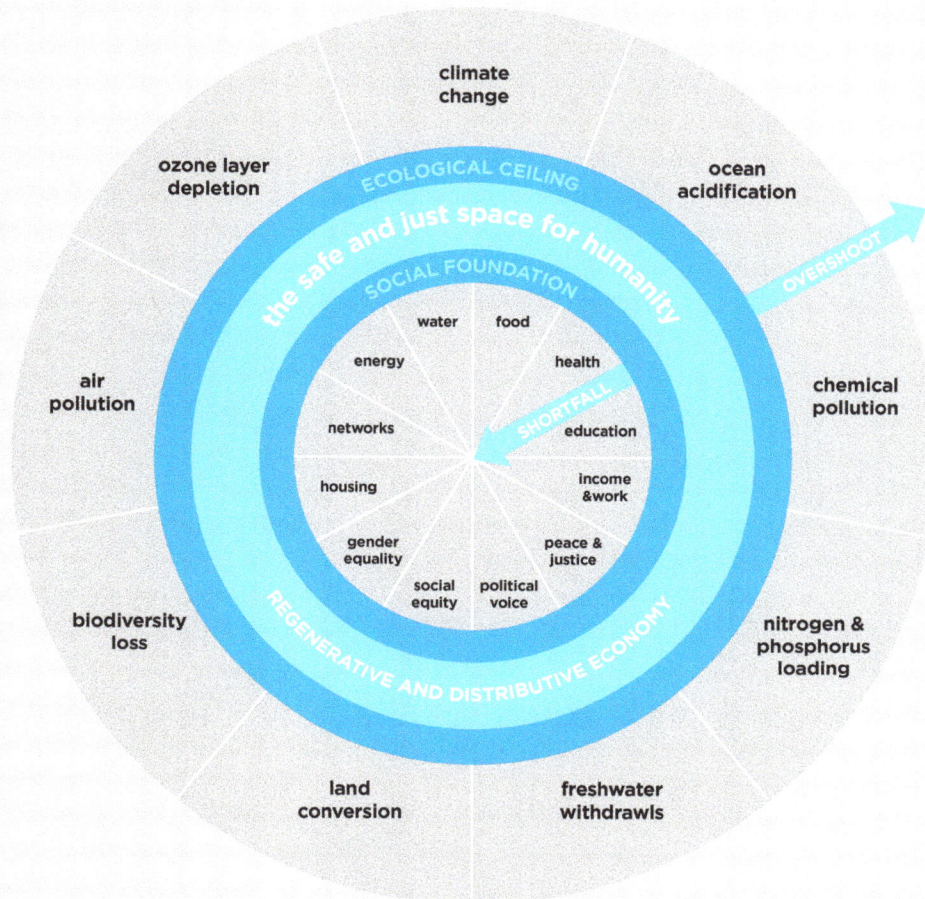

6.3 Connectedness is the gearbox which unleashes the power provided by Choice and Fears

The Internet and Digitalisation are mechanisms that inspire, accelerate and scale new ways of thinking and acting through horizontal (peer-to-peer) communication.

If choice and fears are the engines for the rise of meaning, unfiltered horizontal communication (which we have called Connectedness for short) is the gearbox which transfers power to the wheels of change.

More people than ever before are directly connected over the Web and through mobile devices to anyone, everywhere at any time, and at almost zero marginal cost.

Digitalisation as a technology delivers connectivity at every level. And this in turn inspires, accelerates and scales new ways of thinking and acting.

GLOBAL MOBILE STATISTICS

NUMBER OF MOBILE CONNECTIONS
> 8 000.000.000.000

NUMBER OF UNIQUE MOBILE SUBSCRIBERS
~ 5 000.000.000.000

Source: GSMA
Intelligence
February 2017

Commentators often refer to the fact that we are living in the internet- or digital- age in which new ideas spread rapidly and in so doing can find economic expression faster. For the rise of Meaning as an economic force, the key dynamic is that communication no longer travels vertically through hierarchies in which other people determine what we see. Instead, we communicate directly with each other across heirachical boundaries. This is unfiltered horizontal communication.

Smart phones, tablets and laptops allow us to access and disseminate everything we know, feel and do to everybody, from (practically) everywhere in real time.

A consequence of this is that people can rapidly find "their own tribe" of like-minded individuals in any arena that they find meaningful.

Entrepreneurs act quickly to fill the value opportunities that emerge and the results of their efforts spread around the world with ease and speed.

Especially important is that the Internet and Digitalisation allows businesses to effectively serve the niches at the tail of a demand curve, as well as the major markets at its head.

Called **Long Tail Theory**, this phenomenon was first written about in 2004 in **Wired Magazine** and subsequently turned into a book of the same name by **Chris Anderson**, Wired's then editor-in-chief.

Anderson describes **(Figure 9)** how online, bookstores can stock a range that includes the ability to meet highly specialised interests – something not practical in space-constrained physical stores.

FIGURE 9:
EXAMPLE OF THE LONG TAIL FROM CHRIS ANDERSON'S BOOK OF THE SAME NAME

43%
of Amazon´s sales are books also carried by traditional stores.

57%
of Amazon´s sales are books only carried by Amazon.

Looking from a customer perspective, the Internet and Digitalisation ensure greatly increased potential to find an offering that matches your interests.

And then, when you have found it, you can learn how to use it – not only from the company that offered it, but also from fellow users.

Connectedness creates economic possibilities that even entrepreneurs creating new businesses do not realize exist. The power of YouTube videos to demonstrate how to use pretty much every DIY tool and to make just about anything, was not foreseen by the company's creators whose focus was on music.

Two final observations on connectedness and its relevance to meaning are paradoxical compared with the other remarks in this section:

a. So much communication is digital that it increasingly creates a wellbeing deficit. Digital lives leave people feeling more fragmented and create the need to seek more meaningful human relationships.

b. Many people feel that the current commercial-enabling mechanisms of connectedness create an exploitative dynamic between people as citizens and digital companies. Increasingly people see companies like Google less as useful search engines, and more as exploitative revenue platforms for a "shareholder elite". This perspective increases their risk of becoming stranded as business models, overtaken by more community-based alternatives.

Some of the world's estimated 40 million Trekkies (Star Trek fans) - not everything in the Meaning Economy is necessarily profound.

7. NEW BEHAVIOURS OFFERING NEW OPPORTUNITIES FOR VALUE CREATION

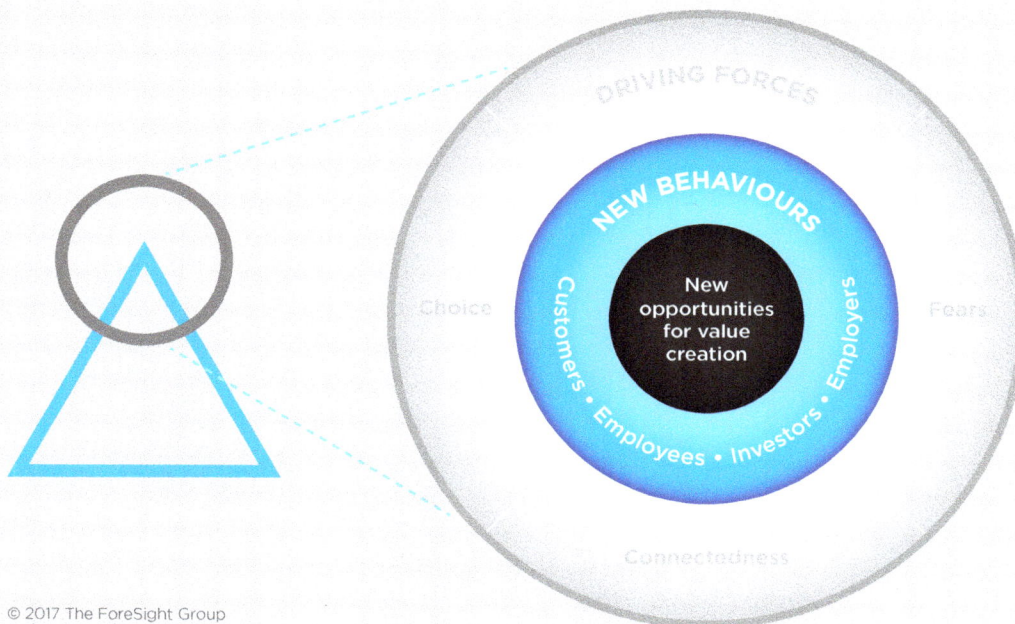

© 2017 The ForeSight Group

Within the Meaningful Economy Lens we have explored the three driving forces of Choice, Fears and Connectedness.

These have created the conditions in which we observe new behaviours in every arena in which people are economically active.

We are changing what we buy, our choices around work, how we set up and operate economic organisations and how we deploy capital.

In short, meaning is changing and will continue to change our behaviours as consumers, employees, employers and investors.

In turn, these new behaviours are creating new opportunities to develop economic value and new threats to value creation as it is achieved today.

In this section we explore new behaviours by both looking at examples and endeavouring to offer perspectives on what is likely to emerge.

New behaviours create new opportunities for value creation by all economic actors but most obviously for organisations.

A starting point to understand the new behaviours that we will discuss is contained in **Figure 10.** In the 20th Century the dominant Western paradigm was the pursuit of happiness (a nice life of material comfort). The rise of the Meaningful Economy is the economic pursuit of a meaningful life.

FIGURE 10:
THE JOURNEY FROM WEALTH TO MEANING

Adapted from Martin Seligman
© 2017 The ForeSight Group.

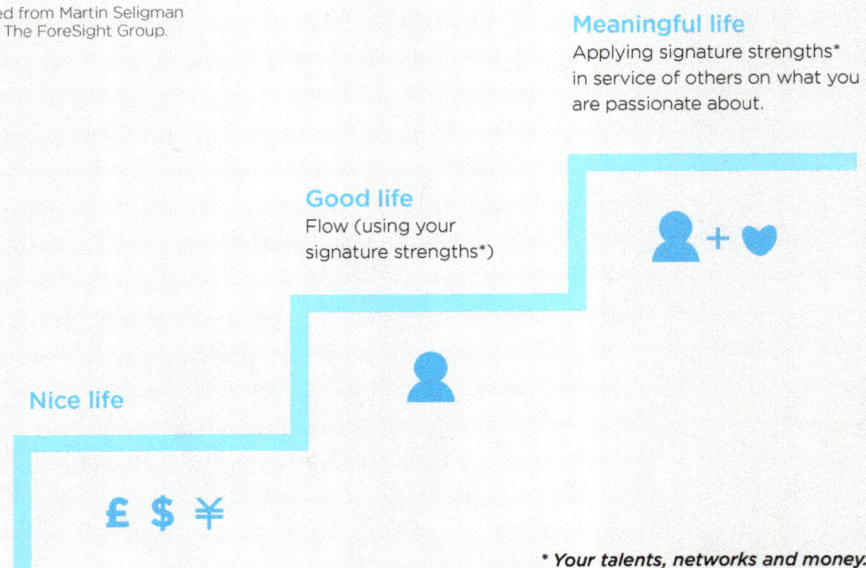

Meaningful life
Applying signature strengths*
in service of others on what you
are passionate about.

Good life
Flow (using your
signature strengths*)

Nice life

£ $ ¥

Your talents, networks and money.

The model was developed by psychologist **Martin Seligman**, and has been adapted and practiced by the **ForeSight Group** to provide a roadmap for people seeking a more fulfilling relationship with their financial wealth. It has general relevance as a guidance system for the personal development of a more meaningful life.

It illustrates a transition from a pursuit of happiness, to a life based on meaning.

In more detail, the three levels in **Figure 10** are:

» **Nice Life:** At the lowest level, wealth is focused on material success and typically deployed on creature comforts. Prior to the rise of the Meaningful Economy it was the focal point of our modern economic system.

» **Good Life:** Stepping up a level, wealth is combined with a person's signature strengths (talents, networks and money) to do something. Here you may experience the sense of flow that is often described by a performance athlete at the top of their game.

» **Meaningful Life:** The final level is when you apply your signature strengths in service of others (the common good) in the arena of something on which you are passionate. At this level you start to experience a meaningful life.

The transition from a nice life to a meaningful life is visible in economic terms in changed behaviour in the four areas of economic activity:

1. **As consumers**
2. **As employees**
3. **As investors**
4. **As creators and managers of businesses**

The Meaningful Economy incorporates areas and activities as diverse as:

» sharing business models
» localism
» mindfulness
» crowd funding
» organic food
» craft beer
» the maker movement
» personal development programmes

A close look at any of these will reveal elements of economic action from more than one aspect of economic activity.

Notwithstanding this, we have identified new behaviours in each main area of economic activity.

Together they illustrate how the rise of the Meaningful Economy offers new places to look for value creation and the way in which it allows a growing number of people to live more meaning-filled lives.

7.1 Meaning defining what we buy, and from who

Meaning is transforming the choices people make in terms of what they buy, where and from who.

In our analysis we have identified three consumer trends in the Meaningful Economy. They are:

» 360 degree company and brand assessment
» Localism
» Sharing

a) 360 degree company and brand assessment

In the consumer society what we buy has more than a utilitarian function. Brands are the signposts for our lives and define who we are and how we fit into the world.

This has been well understood by marketers for a generation.

In the Meaningful Economy customers are widening their expectations of the organisations they support with their wallets.

How a company acts in terms of issues such as paying taxes (eg offshore structures), its environmental track record (explicit and implicit), its employment practices (eg zero hours contracts and its leadership bonus structures) all threaten the ability to be recognised as authentic and therefore to retain its customers and revenue streams.

Examples include customer reaction to online retailers (taxation and employment practices), automotive companies (environmental performance), supermarkets (labour practices) and banks (bonuses).

Meaning as a mechanism of choice creates conditions under which customers, all things being equal, will choose *products* and services that are fair, ecological and ethical, offered by *organisations* that are fair, ecological and ethical.

b) Localism

Localism is a shift to finding products and services that are sourced in and around the immediate area in which people live. It often goes hand in hand with the search for craftsmanship and authenticity. People will search through the supermarket aisles for this week's bargains and then go straight from there to a farmers' market and pay a premium for organic locally grown meat and vegetables.

For special occasions, people will choose restaurants which pride themselves on local sourcing of quality ingredients while at the same time, the same people will eat day-to-day at Subway.

$35.4 BN
Sales in 2014 of men's grooming products, an 8% rise over five years.

19%
Craft beer's share of the overall US beer market

Images: www.shutterstock.com

In the Meaningful Economy, not only what people buy is changing but also how they make buying decisions. Connectedness means that customers will check prices online while standing in a store looking at a product. They will also check how fellow shoppers rate the product or service, sourcing their advice from the crowd.

Another example of the way in which meaning is impacting consumptive buying is found in the rise of **Community Supported Agriculture** (CSA). The first known CSA in Europe, Les Jardins de Cocagne, was founded in 1978 near Geneva, Switzerland. Today in 22 European countries alone there are more than 6,300 CSA initiatives and one million people involved in consuming what they produce.[xxii]

Decentralisation is a wider aspect of the rise of localism as an economic force. Localism has a central idea of building more vibrant local communities in which we can live, work and play.

c) Sharing

Over the past 100 years we have become increasingly individualistic, especially in the Anglo-Saxon economic model that epitomises the 20th century understanding of "success". Being "sufficient unto oneself" became the most important endeavour for many.

In the Meaningful Economy this is changing and a more collective society is emerging. Cooperation and strong networks give meaning to people.

New platforms for sharing talent, lifestyle and the creation of value are appearing. Although we have only seen the beginning of this development they may come to be the dominating infrastructure.

A new norm will emerge in which centralised structures – regardless of whether they are financial, political or technological – will be decentralised into smaller units. Power is redistributed and becomes multi-modal and parallel.

Another aspect of sharing is apparent in a new relationship to ownership. Sharing is not only caring, but cooler than owning.

To a greater extent, a value system governed by sharing moves to the mainstream in the Meaningful Economy. The coming generations are less inclined to feel the need to own their home, their car or even their living room.

Here are five examples:

>> **Room and house sharing** in which people who need somewhere to stay connect with homeowners when they're traveling. The most well known providers here are **AirBnB** and **Couchsurfing**. An interesting new development in this arena is **Commonspace** in Syracuse where halls of residence style living combines private rooms with shared spaces.

>> **Lift and Carsharing** offer the flexibility of private cars without the need to own and maintain a vehicle. **Uber** and **Lyft** let you source a taxi-ride from drivers in their personal vehicles while **Car2Go** and **Zipcar**, provide access to shared vehicles on a pay-by-the-hour basis.

>> **Reselling or just passing on to others things you no longer use** is becoming the norm enabled by online platforms like **Ebay** and **Freecycle**.

>> **Borrowing DIY equipment from Tool Libraries.** These libraries don't lend books, they lend tools to members for DIY, gardening, decorating and machine repair, so that people don't need to own them. A further development of this is virtual tool libraries where people in a village post information onto a platform of the tools they have available in their garage if anybody wants to use them.

>> **Workspaces are becoming open source physical platforms for collaboration** with organisations like **WeWork** (which is approaching 200 offices in 50 cities) enabling shared workspaces between organisations to create both new business collaborations, as well as evolving office space solutions.

UBER

couchsurfing

airbnb

zipcar

ebay

wework

One interesting possible positive outcome of the rise of sharing is a shift towards quality. When people start sharing things, it makes it possible to use quality products that they couldn´t afford if they had to buy them. Products with a focus on quality will potentially have a higher demand in the sharing economy. Another benefit could be that if companies take more responsibility for their products (because the ownership stays with them) then the circular economy and similar movements will become bigger faster.

By contrast, companies with business models based on lower quality mass production with built-in-obsolescence characteristics may struggle in the context of sharing. People will have the potential to buy less stuff for the same level of utility and access higher quality items for lower cost.

We see an increasing number of examples of communities where infrastructure is based on sharing. From micro-living allowing a family to live centrally at an affordable rate to areas where parking is only available for cars that are shared.

In the shared economy smart platforms and booking systems are being developed to allow simple planning for a more flexible life. In the traditional consumption economy too much time was spent maintaining and updating assets and possessions.

The second arena for new behaviours is the world of work. We explore this in the next section.

7.2 Meaning re-shaping our aspirations in the world of work

The Meaningful Economy is creating new behaviours in our roles as employees.

Even the idea of the world of work being primarily about "employment" and being "an employee" is challenged.

In the 20th century, the work environment was driven by the twin notions of a career and of loyal employees. These two ideals created a dominant pattern of commonly understood relationships. Employees worked hard, progressed and were rewarded with salary, job security and a guaranteed pension.

An important background context is that the relative importance of people to a business compared with physical assets has increased dramatically over time.

Figure 11 shows that in 2015, 84% of the value of the S&P 500 comprised intangible assets compared to 17% in 1975.[xxiii]

Technically the monetary value of a firm's intangible-assets is what is left when you deduct the net value of its tangible assets from its market value. But in this context a better way of understanding intangible assets is that they leave the building at 5pm (or whatever time people go home). Intangible assets are about everything that people do beyond the factories, offices, raw material stock, finished products and work in progress. This includes concepts such as brand value and reputation as well as culture and other people-related capabilities.

It's the people, not the stuff that really matters.

In the Meaningful Economy the relationship between employer and employee is changing.

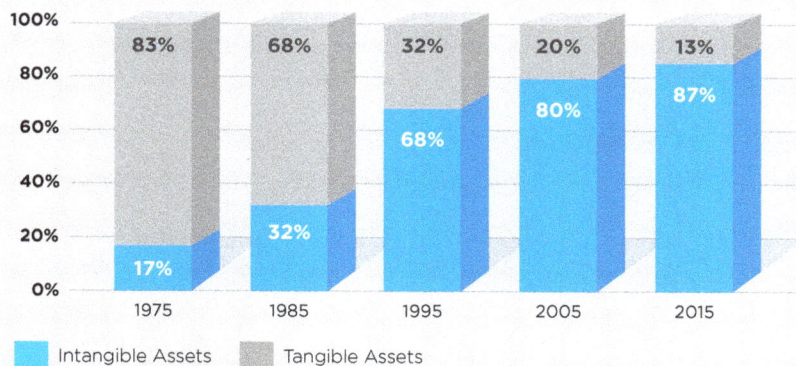

FIGURE 11:
INTANGIBLE ASSETS NOW DOMINATE THE VALUE OF LARGE COMPANIES.

Source:
Ocean Tomo, LLC

We have identified four entry points to exploring new behaviours in the relationship to the world of work:

a) Meaning attracts talent, while its absence sends the best people elsewhere

As meaning becomes more important, attitudes to the desirability of jobs that do not have meaning are changing. The meaningful workplace attracts the greatest talents.

Daniel Pink in his book Drive has highlighted that in work, professional people are motivated by a desire for autonomy, mastery and purpose[xxiv].

Pink's analysis may point to one reason why many commentators have described the financial services sector as being in a long-term systemic crisis, as it appears to demonstrate the lowest orientation towards purpose of any sector of the economy.

Evidence of this can be found in the rise of **Escape the City[xxv]**. This organisation was founded in the financial district of London in 2010. Since then it has grown to more than a quarter of a million members. These are predominantly employees of financial and professional service firms looking for more meaningful work somewhere else.

One large professional service firm in the UK notes that where historically they would expect to lose 20% of their top talent before they reach partner level in the organisation, that figure has risen to 40%.

Growing numbers of high fliers do not see value in working long hours at the expense of families and other activities, doing what they increasingly see as fundamentally meaningless work.

Looking at this from a more positive perspective, the Meaningful Economy allows for the possibility of an economically viable life without a full time job. Skilled professionals find that they can increasingly work freelance and across multiple platforms. This kind of portfolio life is both attractive and increasingly a norm.

At the other end of the economic spectrum the Gig Economy is a labour market characterised by the prevalence of short-term contracts or freelance work, as opposed to permanent jobs.

This has the positive effect of allowing flexibility with regard to employment hours, however the trade off in job security leads many commentators to conclude that people generally take "Gigs" in the absence of permanent opportunities rather than primarily by choice.

However, new research in the UK reveals that the majority of participants in the Gig Economy actually prefer this way of working, with just 14% doing so due to an absence of an alternative.[xxvi]

This finding is in tune with the anecdotal sense that people who make the choice to leave large companies for more independent and flexible work lifestyles rarely go back to the confines of a large organisation by choice, irrespective of the perceived value of job security so often mentioned by those who remain within a company.

Notwithstanding the comments above, it is likely that while the Gig Economy may be changing the world of work, it may be that the high acceptance levels are both a feature of choice and an adaption to the new reality. The larger implications for this include security of accommodation, flexibility and independence of movement/transport. Of itself therefore, the Gig logic isn't a winning concept unless a mechanism is found to offer long-term security, as well as the benefits of short term "flexibility". This is another argument for a Universal Basic Income (see chapter 6 for more discussion on this).

b) Skill transcends knowledge

....

We have often heard that we live in a knowledge-based society. We have been taught that through theoretical education we are able to contribute to growth but also provide ourselves with a good future.

Our studies have shown that Millennials no longer believe in this. We think that they are right. An academic proletariat of "overeducated" people has emerged. They often take menial jobs to secure a livelihood. The problem is a surplus of knowledge and a deficit of skills.

Sites like **Wikipedia** and organisations like **Coursera** which provides more than 2000 academic courses online (and indeed the whole internet itself) efficiently distribute knowledge to an increasing number of people at low cost (or even zero cost). They even allow people to cherry-pick individual courses at different institutions. We are moving to a world where even people from the most disadvantaged societies can access online teachings of leading academic institutions such as **Massachusetts Institute of Education** (MIT). This opens up new possibilities for access to opportunities for people who would otherwise never have had them. In addition to this, apps and **YouTube** increasingly automate access to learning that previously required years of tertiary education in a formal bricks-and-mortar academic institution.

This is the power of what **Nick Ellerby** calls "know how" transcending "know-what".

There is however a health warning in that many traditional academic courses and their technology spin-offs, especially in a business and economic context, continue to perpetuate a status quo worldview from which the search for meaning is usually seeking to move.

In the Meaningful Economy, focus shifts toward skills. Having a skill – whether it is carpentry, surgery or programming – is valued much higher than great theoretical knowledge.

In the skills-based Meaningful Economy, talent and aptitude are more important than formal training. Even greater value is attached to complex talents like service-mindedness, entrepreneurship, artistic expression and a sense for caring.

c) Entrepreneurship takes a central stage

Entrepreneurship is an important part of the Meaningful Economy - a new generation deciding and aspiring to start their own companies or work as independents, rather than working for others.

Systems-wide data on this is not available but evidence can be found in individual Universities. MIT for example, has seen the percentage of students involved in start-ups within three years of graduation rise from under 2% in the 1960s to 12% in the 2010s.[xxvii]

Harvard has reported a sharp increase in students drawn to start-ups with 19% of the graduation class of 2016 joining the technology sector.[xxviii]

The trend to entrepreneurship amongst Millennials may be supported by more affluent Baby-Boomer generation parents providing a safety net for Millennials to "explore" – creating the luxury of time and the resources to experiment. It is not just about Boomer affluence, but also their provision of a good education and the social context and network benefits which increase the ability of their offspring to make different choices.

Further qualitative evidence is visible in, for example, the shift in how business schools promote their offerings and the growth in entrepreneurship courses.

Entrepreneurship is about the freedom and possibility to follow your own passions.

While this trend is strong in the Meaningful Economy, many aspects of the economic system are not supportive of entrepreneurialism as a preferred approach to work.. This is because our societal systems assume the majority of people want a career in a large organisation.

This is especially true within the financial system where for example, obtaining a home loan without a salary slip, is extremely difficult.

Public policy is poorly equipped to handle a world of individuals in permanent employment flux.

d) A new relationship to time

The rise of meaning goes beyond a mechanistic reframing of work. It calls for the opportunity to slow down everyday life while being bombarded with hundreds of impressions.

"

People used to brag and say, 'Oh yeah, 21-hour days, seven days a week for eight months,' that was a badge of honor.

The humble brag is now, 'Oh yeah, I work 9 to 5, I get paid a ton of money, and I have a great life.'

It's green juice from vats in the office and amazing organic iced coffee cold-brewed -- the quality of life.

Kiran Gandhi, Class of 2015 Harvard MBA Graduate[xxix]

Downshifting and the Slow Movement express new behaviours in relation to time.

Kiran Ghandi's observation is visible in the rise of **Downshifting**. Downshifting is about individuals seeking to live simpler lives, escape obsessive materialism and focus life goals on personal fulfilment and building relationships, instead of the all-consuming pursuit of economic success.[xxx]

An indication of the interest in Downshifting is evidenced in **Amazon** having more than 100 books available on the subject.

Similarly the **Slow Movement**[xxxi] advocates a cultural shift toward slowing down life's pace.

It began with **Carlo Petrini's** protest against the opening of a **McDonalds** restaurant in Piazza di Spagna, Rome in 1986 that sparked the creation of the **Slow Food** movement. Since then it has expanded to encompass numerous aspects of life.

Like many behaviours in the Meaningful Economy, our new relationship to time is fragmented, grass roots-driven and bottom up.

This has the effect of making its effects less visible, but its influence is observable in Slow Movement activities including cinema, counselling, education, fashion, food, gardening, interior design, architecture, marketing, media, money, parenting, photography, science, technology, travel and urban design and planning.

Yoga, mindfulness and meditation are all new behaviours inspired by a different relationship to time.

These are new behaviours, in which people seek to stop and feel, to experience what is happening here and now.

In 2012, nearly 10% of U.S. adults participated in yoga, up from 5% a decade earlier.[xxxii]

A 2016 **Fortune** article[xxxiii] captured the way in which Mindfulness and Meditation are now billion dollar sectors of the US economy alone according to research by **IBISWorld,** which breaks out the category from the alternative health care sector.

In addition there are now over one thousand mindfulness apps and a host of wearable gadgets designed to help people shift to another state of consciousness. The same article notes that 22% of employers in the US were set to offer mindfulness training in 2016 and that this could double in 2017

A growing understanding of the importance of spending time in nature and other time outside the office.

Numerous research studies point to the benefits of spending time in nature, with a 2015 Stanford paper on the effects of a walk in nature to counter depression being just one.[xxxiv] With mental health becoming a new frontier of wellbeing in work, the demand for time to do other things will grow.

This new perspective on time is also well-framed by corporate researcher, **Jim Collins** (Jim Collins Live in London, Feb 2017), who notes that even a 1,000 hour day would be insufficient for an executive to do everything that could be done in service of their business. Therefore, in percentage terms (relative to one thousand hours) the choice between an eight-hour working day and a fourteen-hour day is not material relative to the effect of working smarter for a given number of hours chosen. In the Meaningful Economy this perspective will increase in importance as people become less valued for the functional hours worked and more for the actual value delivered.

Time out for community service has a similar logic and is regarded by more and more people as an expectation.

Understanding a new relationship to time is to grasp an ephemeral idea, but the ability to do so and work with its consequences are central to our relationship to work in the Meaningful Economy.

7.3 Meaning impacting investing

The stereotypical view of investing is that it is an activity in which capital is deployed with the purpose of a financial return, constrained only by regulatory frameworks and without moral or ethical considerations.

While this has always been an inaccurate picture, the development of approaches to investing set into the context of meaning has become a growing feature of both the institutional and the individual investment landscapes.

In the Meaningful Economy we see both institutional initiatives and the rise of community-based investing as growing evidence of new behaviours:

a) Institutional investing seeking to align with common good

Institutional investors have been grappling with issues beyond financial return for a generation.

The dominant approach has been the rise of **Environmental, Social and Governance** (ESG) considerations into the investment decision-making process. This is typically a process of either positive or negative screening of investments based on their profile with respect to one or more of these dimensions.

Global initiatives such as the **United Nations Environment Programme – Finance Initiative** (UNEP FI) founded after the 1992 Rio Earth Summit and the **Principles for Responsible Investment** (PRI) which was set up in 2006 to build a network of responsible institutional investors. The PRI's growth has seen its signatories pass 1600 organisations in a decade (**Figure 12**).

FIGURE 12:
THE GROWTH IN SIGNATORIES TO THE UN´S PRINCIPLES FOR RESPONSIBLE INVESTMENT IS A NEW BEHAVIOUR IN THE MEANINGFUL ECONOMY

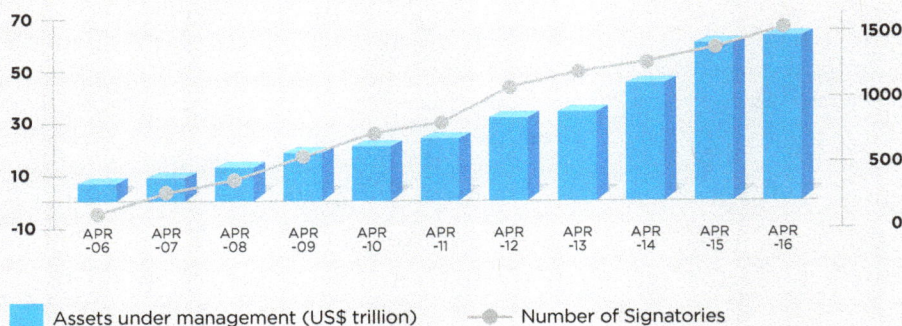

Assets under management (US$ trillion)   Number of Signatories

While the scale of the PRI's development is impressive it should also be noted that it is aspirational in its approach. It does not hold signatory organisations to account beyond reporting. The approach is to create a positive effect through public scrutiny and peer benchmarking, and in so doing also stimulate continuous improvement.

More remarkable than the development of the PRI, is the speed of the emergence of the Divest-Invest Movement. In just two years, financial institutions with more than US$5 trillion in assets under management decided <u>not</u> to invest in fossil fuel energy companies.

The movement originally started as University endowments and has grown to include some seven hundred Institutions and nearly 60,000 individuals in 72 countries.[xl]

Looking into the future of Institutional Investment, the Meaningful Economy is likely to create a much greater change in the value of investments.

This is because of the increased probability that companies will increasingly be forced to internalise costs that currently are carried by nature and society.

In 2013, **Trucost** published a report[xli] on behalf of The Economics of Ecosystems and Biodiversity (TEEB) program which is sponsored by **United Nations** Environmental Program. This report examined the revenues earned by high environmental impact sectors of the economy and compared them with full environmental costs in terms of water use, land use, greenhouse gas emissions, waste pollution, land pollution, and water pollution.

The report found that when you took these externalized environmental costs into effect, industries such as oil, meat, tobacco, mining and electronics were no longer profitable. In many cases the environmental costs were similar to, or exceeded revenues in the sector.

As the Meaningful Economy expands, it is likely that such a disconnect will generate stranded business models and equally create new opportunities for businesses whose business models more fully internalise their environmental (and social) costs.

Another dimension of the investment landscape is that the biggest transfer of wealth in history is under way.

According to Big Path Capital, over the next 35 years an unprecedented US$ 58.7 trillion dollars of wealth will transfer to Millennials and women of all ages. Women will inherit 70% of this wealth and by 2030, two-thirds of the wealth in the United States will be in the hands of women. Given what we know about the rise of the Meaningful Economy, this transition is unlikely to be business-as-usual.

Other examples of new behaviours in a broadly institutional investor context include:
  » **Impact Investing** which combines financial return with a desire to see positive social or environmental impact associated with that investment.
  » **Venture Philanthropy** in which participants deploy their capital to achieve measureable social outcomes/impact using the techniques of venture capital investing.

It is important to note that while the word "Impact" is increasingly used, most measurement remains focused on measuring outcomes.

In our own work at the **ForeSight Group**, we have worked with wealth management companies to build investment platforms for family offices called Passionate Investing. In this approach members of the **Passionate Investment** clubs develop their investment approaches at the intersection between their wealth, their signature strengths as people, social and environmental challenges and what they personally are passionate about. This intersection is all about meaning.

b) Community based investing providing direct connection

In parallel to institutional behaviour two new forms of investing have emerged at a community or individual level. They both use the power of the Internet and digitalisation to directly connect those with capital to those who need it.

  » **Peer-to-peer lending platforms** bring individual borrowers and lenders together cutting out traditional banks. In the UK for example, the three companies **Zopa, Rate Setter** and **Funding Circle** have to date facilitated loans approaching a total of £6 billion.

It is interesting to note in the context of the development of the Meaningful Economy that both Rate Setter and Funding Circle were founded in 2010, the year in which meaning began to develop significance as an economic force.

  » **Crowd funding** is another mechanism through which those in need of funds are matched with those who are willing to provide it. Rather than debt, crowd funding was originally primarily about funding in exchange for rewards or products or a philanthropic contribution with no expectation of monetary or material return. Increasingly it is moving towards equity investing in new ventures.

Together, peer-to-peer lending and crowd funding form the bulk of the alternative finance sector. In Europe, this sector grew from €1.1bn in 2013 to €5.4bn in 2015.[xliii]

In the same year, the market in the Americas was nearly four times the size at €20.3bn and the Asia-Pacific market more than seventeen times bigger than Europe at €90.6bn.

In 2013, all three markets combined were less than €9 billion in total.

While changing patterns of investment are currently relatively small factors in the rise of the Meaningful Economy, financial innovators are building scaled solutions with the potential for disruption to re-balance and restore the role of finance to one of service.

There is certainly plenty of opportunity.

7.4 Meaning is changing how organisations are designed and how they function

In organisations, the most obvious responses to the rise of the Meaningful Economy lie in the creation of products and services that meet the emergent changes in consumer behaviour.

New products and services are however, the tip of the proverbial iceberg.

In this section we will explore three aspects of new behaviours in organisations that may not be so immediately obvious. They are:

a. **Retrofitting** purpose
b. **Reconfiguring** organisational forms
c. **Running differently,** moving from hierarchy to collaborative community

a) Retrofit – Purpose-led business transcends triple bottom line

A major consequence of the rise of meaning as an economic force is the development of businesses which have purpose beyond profit at their core.

Social and ecological relevance to what is emerging from a perspective of Meaning are part of the DNA of purpose-led companies.

Most tellingly, we see a growing number of traditional for-profit listed companies seeking to reinvent themselves around purpose (or at minimum their communications and marketing teams are working hard to portray this as the new reality).

This movement started in the 1980's with the incorporation of social and environmental objectives alongside financial ones to form a triple bottom line.

That was and remains a baseline predicated on doing less harm.

Proactive purpose-led businesses increasingly describe their core mission and objectives in social and environmental terms.

In 2017 the poster child large organisation is **Unilever** that describes its purpose: "[to] make sustainable living commonplace." In its business plans it lives this purpose through a series of clearly articulated social and environmental objectives.[xxxv]

Our ambition goes beyond just changing our own business. We want to change the very way business is done.

We want to use our scale, influence and resources to make a real difference to issues that matter – such as driving women's empowerment, mainstreaming sustainable agriculture, improving access to clean water and sanitation, and eliminating deforestation.

We want to help create 'transformational change' – not simply incremental improvements, but fundamental change to whole systems.

Paul Polman, CEO, *Unilever*

At the collective level, initiatives such as the Ellen MacArthur Foundation's work on the circular economy provide new operating models in relation to environmental issues and in sharing and advancing good practices.[xxxvi]

Similar initiatives exist around social issues such as Human Rights.

Such initiatives however remain fragile as long as the structure of companies allow old patterns to re-emerge under stress. And even the best businesses experience a cycle of good times and bad.

New organisational forms are Meaningful Economy responses to these structural problems and we examine them in the next section.

b) Reconfigure - New organisational forms

A picture of private and public shareholder companies informed the 20th century view of business with profit as the one-and-only yardstick of success.

There were of course, long-established alternatives such as customer, producer and employee co-operatives and provident societies.

However in recent years, we have seen the growth of new kinds of purpose-led businesses including social enterprises, community interest companies and benefit corporations.

In the Meaningful Economy, in addition to what a company offers and how it brings that into being, the design of the organisation becomes either an enabler or disabler of its ability to create value.

This is creating new company structures and legal frameworks and a blurring of roles between for-profit and not-for-profit organisations.

An example of this is the emergence of **Benefit Corporations (B Corps).**

B Corps, operate within a certification framework in which they explicitly define themselves as purpose-driven and in the service of stakeholders, not only shareholders.

In six years to 2014, some 1,000 organisations registered as B Corps. That number doubled in the ensuing two years to pass the 2000 mark at the start of 2017.[xxxvii]

Another more radical approach founded in organisational design is the growing community of companies inspired by the work of **Christian Felber**[xxxviii] on the Economy for the Common Good. **Common Good Corporations** focus on achieving an overall contribution to the common good rather than by a move away from doing less harm.

If organisational structures are the hardware, parallel new behaviours are appearing in the "software" of management systems.

c) Run differently - From hierarchy to self-managed teams

Another emergent new behaviour is the growing interest in management systems based on new ways of thinking about how people work together.

A prominent example of this is **Frederic Laloux's** work on what has become called the Teal Paradigm of organizations operating from a higher level of human consciousness.[xxxix]

Key aspects include self-management, wholeness and evolutionary (rather than fixed) organizational purpose. The organization is understood as a complex, adaptive living system to nurture rather than as a machine to optimize.

Examples of Teal Organisations include:

Buurtzorg: a Netherlands-based healthcare nonprofit

FAVI: a brass foundry in France, which produces (among other things) gearbox forks for the automotive industry, and has about 500 employees.

Morning Star: a U.S.-based tomato processing company with 400 to 2,400 employees (depending on the season) and a 30 to 40 percent share of the North American market.

Patagonia: a manufacturer of climbing gear and outdoor apparel; based in California and employing 1,300 people, it is dedicated to being a positive influence on the natural environment.

Resources for Human Development (RHD): a 4,000-employee nonprofit social services agency operating in 14 states in the U.S., providing services related to addiction recovery, homelessness, and mental disabilities.

Sun Hydraulics: a maker of hydraulic cartridge valves and manifolds, with factories in the U.S., the U.K., Germany, and Korea employing about 900 people.

The lens of meaning enables us to make identify a coherent narrative behind new behaviours in our four economic roles as customers, employees, investors and managers.

Having explored examples of these behaviours in this section, the authors anticipate that the reader will start to see others in their own contexts. They represent a significant opportunity for individuals to lead more meaning-filled lives and for organisations to create enhanced value.

In the next section we offer some further reflections on other aspects of the Meaningful Economy.

8. FURTHER REFLECTIONS

This analysis concentrates on the organisational and business consequences of the rise of the Meaningful Economy, but we recognise that its ramifications are also powerful at the level of the individual and within a wider societal context.

The Meaningful Economy is still at an early stage, but we think it will grow in importance.

In just a few years it is our view that it will influence all parts of society.

The Meaningful Economy is about a new kind of development where economic activity is restored to its role as an enabler of progress, not the outcome.

In this section of closing reflections we have captured our thoughts on some issues not covered elsewhere.

8.1 More attention on new metrics

One of the by-products of the rise of the Meaningful Economy is interest in new measurements to indicate economic success. Today, there is lively discussion about the relevance of GDP as an indicator and its replacement with common good and/or wellbeing measurements. The most prominent of these are:

> » **The Human Development Index** (HDI) which ranks countries in a composite statistic of life expectancy, education, and per capita income indicators, into four tiers of human development has been around for 25 years but is enjoying new attention.

> » **The World Happiness Report** which surveys the state of global happiness. The first report was published in 2012 and although it uses the term Happiness, its orientation is towards the common good of meaning rather than the personal focus of happiness.

The Meaningful Economy will create an increased focus on new measurements as it grows.

8.2 The driving forces which give rise to the Meaningful Economy have also unleashed new behaviours that are not positive

The driving forces (choice, fears and connectedness) have not only created the conditions for the rise of the Meaningful Economy. They have also unleashed behaviours that are not positive.

Leading thinkers in psychology and human development such as **Ken Wilber, Richard Barrett** (and before them **Clare W. Graves**) have long recognised that our level of consciousness evolves both within individuals over time, and across generations.

This is generally an enabling phenomenon in which we move from an "I" focus, through a focus on "we" (my family, community, company, town, country), to "all of us" (human kind, the planet, nature, the cosmos). **However when individual development is blocked, it can give rise to negative values and behaviours.**

The driving forces of the Meaningful Economy are capable of supporting and scaling the development of negative values and behaviours as well as they can support and scale a positive outcome.

Regressive behaviour is less evident in economic terms than it is in a political context, but it is still visible.

Examples of negative economic behaviours enabled and scaled by the same forces enabling the Meaningful Economy include child abuse tourism, post-truth publishing and the trade in endangered wildlife and plants.

8.3 Anti-institutionalism and the crisis of trust in leadership

The force of anti-institutionalism is inspired by a search for something that works in response to a sense that very little today does actually work at the level of making people or societies whole.

It is a very primal response driven by a sentiment that says "anything is better than this lot".

Anti-institutionalism is leading to a questioning of everything – especially the most prominent institutions of our time.

These include nation-state political systems and the major political parties, large corporations, assumed value systems and the very idea of what constitutes "progress".

The crisis of trust in leadership is deep and universal.

Writing in the 2017 **Edelman Trust Barometer**[xliii] **Richard Edelman** concludes:

> *The growing storm of distrust is powerful and unpredictable. Trust in institutions has evaporated to such an extent that falsehood can be misconstrued as fact, strength as intelligence, and self-interest as social compact.*
>
> *This has been a slow-motion meltdown, an angry delayed recognition of permanent decline in economic and social status by those who have not kept pace with globalization and dramatic technological change.*

Photo: www.edelman.com

The Barometer records for the first time that trust in all institutions (business, politics, NGO's) has fallen below 50% in two thirds of the countries surveyed.

8.4 Meaning versus Happiness

During our work on this analysis, we explored the question of whether there was a fundamental difference between meaning and happiness and whether it matters.

There is and it does.

Once again we found the best insight in the work of Baumeister and his fellow researchers[xliv] who concluded:

» While happiness may satisfy wants and needs, it seems largely irrelevant to a meaningful life.
» Happiness involves being focused on the present, whereas meaning involves thinking more about the past, present, and future — and the relationship between them.
» Meaning is derived from giving to other people; happiness comes largely from what they give to you.
» Meaningful lives involve stress and challenges which happy lives do not.
» Self-expression is important to meaning, but not to happiness.

8.5 The Meaningful Economy is not THE truth

Our exploration of the rise of the Meaningful Economy is offered in the spirit of parallel truths. This is not (we hasten to add) the same thing as Post Truth! It is instead that we do not see the Meaningful Economy as a universal truth that can provide answers to everything. Instead, it is an informative framework around which more insightful understanding can be built and better decisions made. It exists alongside other ways of understanding the economic world with a holistic approach where new insights transcend and include prior understandings.

Our insights are also offered in the knowledge that, as individuals, organisations and societies at large expand their recognition and understanding of the Meaningful Economy, collective ability to engage with it, new insights and with them new possibilities for value creation will emerge.

8.6 The Meaningful Economy presents another tunnel-through opportunity for the developing world

In the Developed World, amongst what **Clem Sunter**[xlv] calls the "rich old millions", the Meaningful Economy is a signpost to a future beyond consumption as the goal.

While for many this is attractive, it creates a significant challenge for rich countries whose societies have been built on the premise that economic growth is a universal panacea. For what Sunter calls the "poor young billions" of the Developing World, it represents an exciting opportunity.

There is real potential to tunnel straight through the mountain of a resource-intensive consumer society to something altogether more complete and satisfying (as well as socially and ecologically sustainable).

8.7 The Meaningful Economy and the United Nations Sustainable Development Goals (SDG's)

On September 25th 2015, working together at the United Nations, the world adopted a set of goals to end poverty, protect the planet, and ensure prosperity for all as part of a new sustainable development agenda.

Each goal has specific targets to be achieved over the next 15 years.

SUSTAINABLE DEVELOPMENT GOALS

1 NO POVERTY
2 ZERO HUNGER
3 GOOD HEALTH AND WELL-BEING
4 QUALITY EDUCATION
5 GENDER EQUALITY
6 CLEAN WATER AND SANITATION
7 AFFORDABLE AND CLEAN ENERGY
8 DECENT WORK AND ECONOMIC GROWTH
9 INDUSTRY, INNOVATION AND INFRASTRUCTURE
10 REDUCED INEQUALITIES
11 SUSTAINABLE CITIES AND COMMUNITIES
12 RESPONSIBLE CONSUMPTION AND PRODUCTION
13 CLIMATE ACTION
14 LIFE BELOW WATER
15 LIFE ON LAND
16 PEACE AND JUSTICE STRONG INSTITUTIONS
17 PARTNERSHIPS FOR THE GOALS

For the goals to be reached, everyone needs to do their part: organisationally this includes governments, the private sector and civil society.

The Meaningful Economy offers a mechanism through which policy makers, individuals and organisations and people everywhere can activate their economic power to support and accelerate the process of achieving the SDG's.

This is because it is a grass roots movement which firmly points in the same direction as the SDG's. Symbiotically, the 17 SDG's represent a measurement system that can be used to quantify the pace of the development of the Meaningful Economy.

In the Meaningful Economy, we see the possibility of a change in the overall narrative. This may be the beginning of a story of an economic future that moves beyond a focus on GDP growth. We are laying a platform for values-driven development and it is happening bottom-up, not top down.

It therefore has the potential to offer an alternative focus to the GDP-dominated, monetary economic worldview that has provided the overarching framework for economic policy in the past two generations.

The Meaningful Economy is a more holistic view. It puts the whole and individual human being, set in the context of all life and the greater questions of existence, at the centre of the economy rather than the systems and institutions we create.

Policy support for the development of the Meaningful Economy will contribute to addressing the deeper concerns changing the way people act as voters and citizens and naturally align them with the Sustainable Development Goals.

After all, in the pursuit of meaning, spending the next fifteen years using our economic choices to end poverty, protect the planet and ensure prosperity for all is more than a good start.

"

The left versus right political model is irrelevant. The main struggle is between global and national. We therefore need a compelling new political model and completely new ways of even thinking of politics.

The essence is that we now have a global ecology and economy, but national politics. This is ineffective. The political system is no longer in control of the forces that control our lives.

We either need to nationalise the global economy or globalise the political system.

Yuval Harari, Author of *Sapiens*

9. ABOUT THE AUTHORS

MARK DREWELL Senior Partner, The ForeSight Group

mark.drewell@foresight.se

Mark is an internationally recognised thought and action leader on the development of organisations and leadership for the 21st century. Oxford educated, at the age of 27 he co-created a business community forum in South Africa that was replicated over 4 000 times and became a vital component of the peaceful transition of power to **Nelson Mandela**.

Prior to becoming a partner in the **ForeSight Group** he was the Founding Chairman and then CEO of the **Globally Responsible Leadership Initiative** – building a coalition of companies and business schools on all continents focused on developing the next generation of globally responsible business leaders. In his business career he served for a decade on the Executive Committee of **Barloworld**, a 35 000 employee industrial group with operations in 32 countries.

He has also served as board member and chaired the global conferences of the **IABC**, the professional association of 13 000 business communicators.

BJÖRN LARSSON CEO, The ForeSight Group

....

bjorn.larsson@foresight.se

Björn has a background as an economist, journalist and diplomat. He is today CEO of **the ForeSight Group**, which was founded in 1979 and has worked with some 150 companies and offered 3.5 million employees opportunities to contribute to corporate innovation and renewal.

ForeSight´s entrepreneurial approach to speed up and leverage the achievements of major ambitions includes Passionate Investments, which was launched in partnership with the oldest bank in Scandinavia. Passionate Investments was recognized for its innovative approach by **President Bill Clinton** at a plenary closing of the Clinton Global Initiative AGM in New York.

Björn is also:
» a founding member of the **Global Impact Investment Network**,
» a member of the Global Advisory Board to **PVBLIC** (New York),
» a fellow of the **Royal Society for the Encouragement of the Arts** (RSA), UK, and the **Aspen Institute**, US.

Since its inception, he has served as an International Ambassador for **The World´s Children´s Prize** helping it become the world´s largest empowerment initiative on rights and democracy for the next generation active in over 100 countries. Five Nobel laureates including **Nelson Mandela** (posthumous) and **Joseph Stiglitz** are patrons.

10. AFTERWORD

During the time we have worked on this paper, we have sought advice from many people around the world – both thought leaders and practitioners whose opinions we respect.

Normally under such circumstances, a pattern of response emerges and in that pattern it is easy to identify gaps and opportunities for further development.

Fascinatingly in this case, the responses and feedback displayed no particular pattern beyond the shared sense that we are on to something important and that this multi-dimensional narrative merits development in its scope, depth and application.

In that regard, we are now looking at a number of mechanisms to enable what we have discovered to be more widely accessible.

To do this we are:
1. accepting public speaking engagements,
2. advising organisations who see the potential to create value through the lens of meaning, and
3. developing a financial platform for the deployment of capital (investing) in the Meaningful Economy.

We are also developing other communication platforms.

Accordingly, we warmly encourage you to get in touch if either any of these arenas are of interest to you or if you have your own insights and experiences on the Meaningful Economy which can contribute to our growing picture of its development.

 William Ford Gibson, the American-Canadian writer who coined the term "cyberspace" said:

"The future is already here, it is just not very evenly distributed."

In terms of meaning as an economic force, he is certainly right. By shining a light on it, we hope it will enable you to contribute to making your own life, and the lives of others, more meaningful.

MARK DREWELL

mark.drewell@foresight.se

BJÖRN LARSSON

bjorn.larsson@foresight.se

11. ENDNOTES

i Frankl, Viktor, **"The Unheard Cry for Meaning"**, Simon & Schuster, New York, ISBN 978-1-4516-6438-6, 2011

ii The ForeSight Group's founders, Sven Atterhed, Lennart Boksjö and Gustaf Delin shared an office in Washington D.C. with John Naisbitt. Naisbitt was one of the many global thought leaders who have been ForeSight friends and collaborators over nearly four decades.

iii Peter Majanen's company Quattroporte (www.quattroporte.se) has developed a proprietorial analytical model that makes it possible to trace what has been written on the Internet and in social media and convert unstructured text into analysable quantitative data. The database consists of 100 million pages of information and 1 billion tweets. In this assembly of ones and zeros we can follow the birth and growth of trends but also their ebbing and demise. Peter Majanen was formerly the Swedish Head of Analysis, Gallup, Director of Development, Demoskop, as well as a Director at Kreab Gavin Andersson.

iv http://www.gartner.com/technology/topics/data-analytics.jsp: Big Data is high-volume, high-velocity and/or high-variety information assets that demand cost-effective, innovative forms of information processing that enable enhanced insight, decision making, and process automation.

v Principle Component Analysis confirmed that there were a statistically correlated series of developments emerging in parallel and in a common direction. The graph below plots a selection of these. They show a strong statistical correlation in their parallel emergence.

Sharing Economy, Entertainment, Debt-free, Impact investment and Circular Economy. 2000–2016. 100=Average for the world

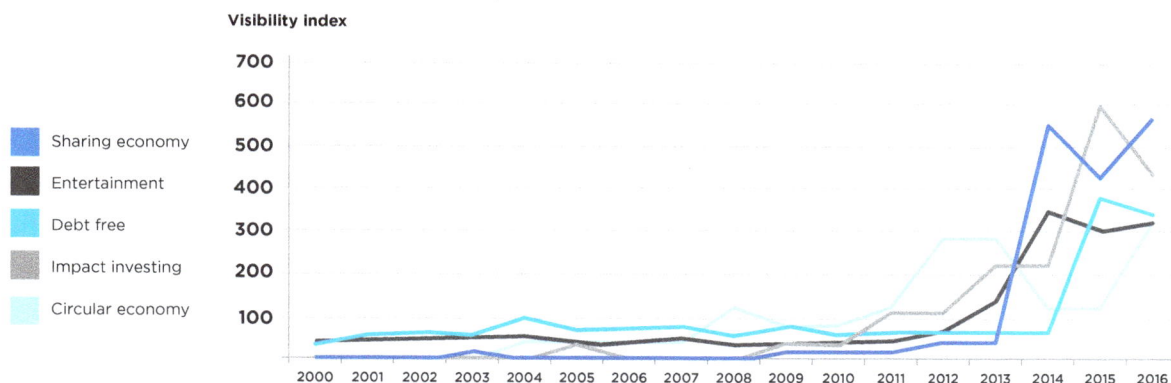

Visibility index

Legend: Sharing economy, Entertainment, Debt free, Impact investing, Circular economy

vi Richard Barrett is an author, speaker and internationally recognised thought leader on the evolution of human values in business and society. He is the founder and chairman of the Barrett Values Centre®, a Fellow of the World Business Academy and Former Values Coordinator at the World Bank.

vii **"Millennials: Changing Consumer Behaviour"**, Goldman Sachs, May 2015

viii The tipping point is that magic moment when an idea, trend, or social behaviour crosses a threshold, tips, and spreads like wildfire. Gladwell, Malcolm, **"The Tipping Point: How little things can make a big difference"**, ISBN-10: 0349113467, Abacus; 2000

ix Roy F Baumeister is Francis Eppes Eminent Scholar and Professor of Psychology at Florida State University. Of particular relevance is the paper: **Some key differences between a happy life and a meaningful life**, Roy F. Baumeister, Kathleen D. Vohs, Jennifer L. Aaker & Emily N. Garbinsky, The Journal of Positive Psychology Vol. 8 , Iss. 6, 2013

x Pine, B. Joseph II and Gilmore, James, **"Welcome to the Experience Economy"**, Harvard Business Review, 1 July 1998

xi United States Department of Agriculture Research Service, International Macroeconomic Data Set published online

xii Norberg, Johan, **"Progress: Ten Reasons to Look Forward to the Future"**, ISBN-10: 1780749503, 2016

xiii Hawking, Stephen, **"This is the most dangerous time for our plant, published in The Guardian, 1 December 2016**

xiv Frey Carl Benedikt and Osborne, Mchael A., **"The future of employment: how susceptible are jobs to computerisation?"**, report published by the Oxford Martin Programme on Technology and Employment, Oxford Martin School, University of Oxford, September 17, 2013

xv Brynjolfsson, Erik, Director of the MIT Initiative on the Digital Economy, **"When the Machines Take Our Jobs, Will We Be Freed?"**, published online in The Atlantic CITYLAB, 17 February 2017

xvi Bort, Ryan , **"Elon Musk Says Governments Will Have To Introduce 'Universal Basic Income' For Unemployed"**, published online by Newsweek, 13 February 2017

xvii Hardoon, Deborah, **An Economy for the 99%: It's time to build a human economy that benefits everyone, not just the privileged few"**, Oxfam, ISBN 978-0-85598-861-6, 16 January 2017

xviii Richardson, John H. 7 July 2015 **"When the End of Human Civilization Is Your Day Job"**, published online by Esquire,

xix Cambridge University Institute for Sustainability Leadership, Presentation to ForeSight clients, March 2013

xx Steffen et al, **"Planetary Boundaries: Guiding human development on a changing planet"**, Science Vol. 347 no. 6223, 2015.

xxi **"Migrant crisis: Migration to Europe explained in seven charts"**, published online by BBC News, 4 March 2016

xxii Volz et al, **"Overview of Community Supported Agriculture in Europe"**, ISBN: 976-2-9551195-5-6, May 2016

xxiii see note one above

xxiv Pink, Daniel H., **"Drive: the surprising truth about what motivates us"**, ISBN-10: 1594484805, Riverhead Books, April 2011

xxv Source: Escape the City, published on their website, February 2017

xxvi **"To gig or not to gig? Stories from the modern economy"**, CIPD survey report, March 2017

xxvii Roberts, Edward B., Murray, Fiona, Kim, Daniel J., **"Entrepreneurship and Innovation at MIT Continuing Global Growth and Impact"**, MIT Sloan School of Management, December 2015

xxviii Harvard Business School website, Data and Statistics, March 2017

xxix **"For Harvard MBS's congrats on a bank job really means I'm-sorry"**, published online by Bloomberg, 6 August 2015

xxx Source: Wikipedia, Downshifting

xxxi Source: Wikipedia, Slow Movement

xxxii Clarke et al, **"Trends in the Use of Complementary Health Approaches Among Adults: United States, 2002–2012"**, U.S. Department of Health and Human Services, Centers for Disease Control and Prevention National Center for Health Statistics, National Health Statistics Reports No. 79, 10 February 2015

xxxiii Wieczner, J, **"Meditation Has Become A Billion-Dollar Business"**, published online by Fortune, Mar 12, 2016

xxxiv Bratmana, Gregory N. et al, **"Nature experience reduces rumination and subgenual prefrontal cortex activation"**, PNAS vol 112 No.28, July 2015

xxxv **"Sustainable Growth: Value + Values"**, Unilever website, March 2017

xxxvi **"What is the Circular Economy?"** Ellen MacArthur Foundation website, March 2017

xxxvii www.bcorporation.net

xxxviii Felber, Christian, **"CHANGE EVERYTHING // Creating an Economy for the Common Good"**, Zed Books Ltd, ISBN-10: 1783604727, June 2015

xxxix Laloux, Frederic, **"Reinventing Organizations: A Guide to Creating Organizations Inspired by the Next Stage in Human Consciousness"**, Nelson Parker, SBN-10: 2960133501, February 2014

[xl] **"The Global Fossil Fuel Divestment and Clean Energy Investment Movement"**, published by Arabella Advisors, December 2016

[xli] Sughdev, P. et al, **"Natural Capital At Risk: The Top 100 Externalities of Business"**, Trucost study on behalf of the TEEB for Business Coalition, April 2013

[xlii] Zhang, Brian et al, **"Sustaining Momentum - The 2nd European Alternative Finance Industry Report"**, University of Cambridge, Judge Business School, Centre for Alternative Finance, September 2016

[xliii] Edelman Trust Barometer, 2017

[xliv] see note IX above

[xlv] Clem Sunter, strategist, scenario expert and former business executive

www.ingramcontent.com/pod-product-compliance
Lightning Source LLC
Chambersburg PA
CBHW040155200326
41521CB00022B/2613